A Kid's Guide to Awesome Duct Tape Projects

A Kid's Guide to Awesome Duct Tape Projects

How to Make Your Own Wallets, Bags, Flowers, Hats, and Much, Much More!

Instructables.com

Sky Pony Press
New York

Sky Pony Press books may be purchased in bulk at special discounts for sales promotion, corporate gifts, fund-raising, or educational purposes. Special editions can also be created to specifications. For details, contact the Special Sales Department, Sky Pony Press, 307 West 36th Street, 11th Floor, New York, NY 10018 or info@skyhorsepublishing.com.

Sky Pony® is a registered trademark of Skyhorse Publishing, Inc.®, a Delaware corporation.

Visit our website at www.skyponypress.com.

10 9 8 7 6 5 4 3 2 1

This product conforms to CPSIA 2008

Library of Congress Cataloging-in-Publication Data is available on file.

Cover design by Owen Corrigan
Cover photo credit Instructables.com

Paperback ISBN: 978-1-5107-5177-4
Hardcover ISBN: 978-1-62914-801-4
E-book ISBN: 978-1-62914-810-6

Printed in China

TABLE OF CONTENTS

CLOTHING, JEWELRY, AND ACCESSORIES

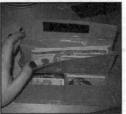

HATS

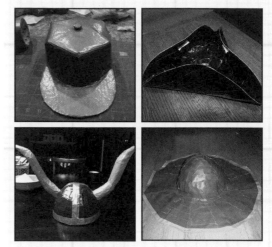

SPORTS, GAMES, AND OUTDOOR ACTIVITIES

SCHOOL AND OFFICE SUPPLIES

CREATURES

EXTRA FUN

Introduction

Duct tape—it's the handyman's secret weapon. It can attach, cover, support, or seal its way through any project, and now it's your greatest tool in making all kinds of fun things!

Deck yourself out from head to toe with duct tape flip flops, make a stylish wallet, or dazzle with a waterproof sunhat. Once you've finished making accessories for yourself, look around your home and see what could use some duct tape enhancements!

In *A Kid's Guide to Awesome Duct Tape Projects*, we've gathered an amazing collection of duct tape projects that are great for kids and DIYers of all ages! All the projects in this book have been carefully crafted by makers just like you who want to find the exciting in the ordinary! Each of these projects was made by a member of Instructables.com, a community of makers who share the passion of wanting to create and share those creations with the world.

Join us as we give you just a small sample of the amazing duct tape creations possible from our community. Explore the world of duct tape in its many colors and designs and see what you can make!

—Nicole Smith
(Penelopy Bulnick)

Flowers

Duct Tape Lily
By knewhall
www.instructables.com/id/
Duct-Tape-Lily/

This duct tape lily is a super simple variation on the classic duct tape rose. It's pretty simple, but a little messier than the very symmetrical rose design, as it requires gathering each of the petals as you attach them. It's okay if it looks a little rough as you assemble it, because one of the last steps is to cover up all your folds with a single strip of long white tape that tightens and smoothes your petal layers.

Step 1: Gather Your Supplies
You will need:
- Colored duct tape (white, yellow, green)
- Wire coat hanger
- Scissors
- Wire cutters

Step 2: Make the Stem of the Flower
Using the coat hanger, cut a long and straight "stem" from one side of the hanger. Each coat hanger should make 2 stems.

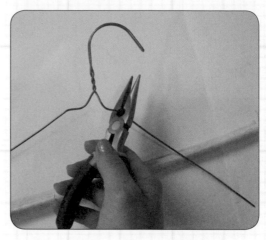

Step 3: Make the Inner "Pistil" of the Flower
Cut a 2-inch segment of yellow duct tape. Cut into 2 strips lengthwise. Repeat twice to make a total of 3 pistils. Save the fourth strip, unfolded. Fold the corners of each strip to make a point at each of the ends.

Step 4: Make the First Pistil
Take the first folded strip and wrap it around the wire stem to make the innermost pistil.

Step 5: Make and Attach 2 More Pistils

Take the next 2 yellow strips (with pointed, folded ends) and wrap them around themselves, unattached to the flower. With the fourth strip of yellow tape, attach the 2 pistils to the pistil anchored to the wire stem. You now have the center of your flower!

Step 7: Attach the Petals to the Stem

Using the exposed sticky tape, affix the petal to the stem, holding it at an angle. Gather slightly the tape as you wrap it around the stem so that it is a little loose and the petal stands up and out. Repeat this process several times with 4 to 5 more petals. You can stagger your petals up around on the back to make a more lily-like petal arrangement. Once you have added all the petals, cover up the gathers on the backside of the flower with a couple of strips of white tape cut super thin.

Step 8: Color/Cover Your Stem

Now that all your petals are made, you will want to make your stem green by wrapping it in thin strips of green duct tape.

Step 6: Make the Petals of the Lily

Now it's time to make the white petals. Cut a 3-inch strip of white duct tape. Fold the corners lengthwise to make a wide point. Make sure to leave adequate tape exposed at the bottom to attach the petal to the stem. I like to make several petals at a time so that I can affix several in a row.

Step 9: Add Outer Leaves

Now that your flower is done, add green tape to make the outer green leaves. You will make these the exact same way you made the white petals.

Step 10: It's All Done!

A finished lily! It may not be perfect, but you get the idea. Mine tend to each turn out differently, and I wind up using different numbers of petals depending on how the shape of the flower is coming along. After a few, you'll get a feel for where to stick each petal to build the shape that you want. Happy lily making!

Realistic Duct Tape Rose

By DIY Hacks and How Tos
www.instructables.com/id/Realistic-Duct-Tape-Rose/

This project is my attempt at creating a duct tape rose that is as realistic as possible.

Step 1: Materials

- Red duct tape (about 3–4 feet per rose)
- Green duct tape (about 2–3 feet per rose)
- Red marker
- Green marker
- Floral wire (or other stiff wire; about 10 feet)

Step 2: Making the Petals

To form the petals, start by cutting off a piece of wire that is about a foot long and a piece of red duct tape about 4 inches long. Stick the wire to the duct tape so that they overlap about one-third of the length of the duct tape. Then fold the duct tape over the end of the wire and stick the 2 sides together. This will form the basic structure of the petal. Cut the petal to shape by trimming the sides and rounding off the end. If you don't want the white adhesive to show, use the marker to color in the cut edges. Repeat this process for a total of 10 petals. You will want to make a variety of sizes. In a real rose, the inner petals are smaller than the outer petals. Copying that structure helps you to get the shape right.

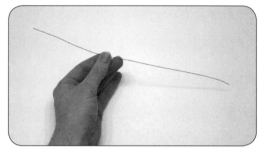

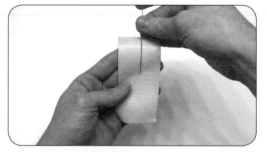

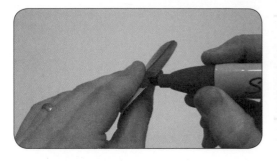

Step 3: Shaping the Petals

Start forming the rose by taking the smallest petal and loosely rolling it into a tube. Then with each additional petal there are few extra things that you need to do to shape them. Each petal should be offset from the previous one in a spiral. To make the petals gently curl around the center, pinch the tape as you wrap it. This makes the bottom of the petal a little narrower than the middle, making it a little more rounded. The rest of the shaping is done by bending the wire. Fold out the tip and press it towards the stem. This causes the middle to bulge and gives it its vertical curve.

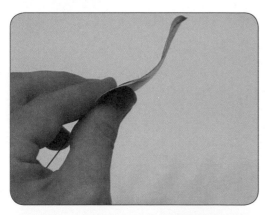

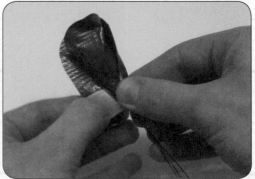

Step 4: Forming the Bud

Repeat the previous steps with each additional petal. After adding a petal, stop and make adjustments as needed. The final shape is determined by the kind of bud that you want to make. Younger buds have the petals more tightly wrapped and closer together. Mature buds are fuller and more spread out. It helps if you have a reference picture nearby while you are shaping the rose.

Step 5: Making the Stem

Once all the petals are attached, form the stem by tightly twisting all the wires together. To cover the stem, cut off a piece of green duct tape the same length as the exposed wire. Then roll the stem onto the duct tape. You may need to cut some slots in the top end to help it roll on straight

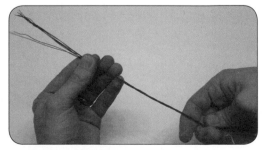

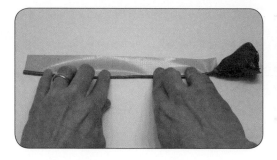

Step 6: Adding the Sepals

The last thing to add is the sepals. Cut off a 3-inch piece of green duct tape and fold one end over, similar to the way the petals were made. From this, cut out a small triangle with the exposed tape at the base. After coloring the edges with the green marker, attach it to the base of the flower. Repeat this for a total of 5 sepals. Try to keep them as evenly spaced as possible.

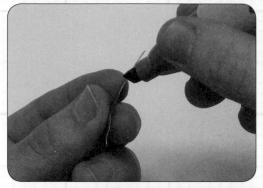

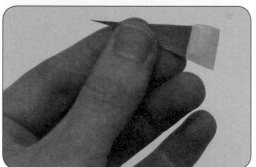

Step 7: Completed Rose

Do some final shaping and your duct tape rose is complete. Each rose will take about 30 minutes to make. It is not a quick crafting project, but it is fun. You can use the basic principles to make other flowers as well. Feel free to experiment and try out different designs

Duct Tape Trick Clown Flower

By airsoftsniper12
www.instructables.com/id/
Duck-Tape-Trick-Clown-Flower/

Yup, it's a clown flower. What's a clown flower? You know, one of the flowers that clowns use to squirt people in the face! I will show you how to make one, with duct tape!

Step 1: Materials

You will need few materials that will cost you little to no money!

- Duct tape in whatever color you want
- A straw, any size you want
- Ruler
- Scissors
- A water bottle

Step 2: The Petals

Making the petals is easy. All you have to do is cut 2-inch pieces of duct tape then fold them to form a triangle. You will want about 10 or 15 of these, or more. That's it. Easy, right?

Step 3: Cutting the Straw

Next, all you have to do is cut a straw. I cut mine to be about 5 inches. You can cut it shorter, or leave it the original length. It's all up to you. After you cut the straw, you are going to cut a long piece of duct tape in half. Next, wrap it around the top of the straw.

If you want you can add another straw and make the stem longer.

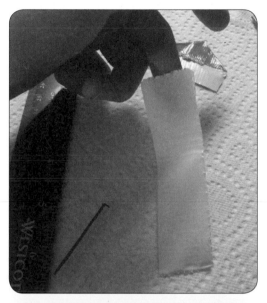

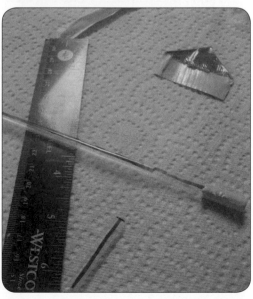

Step 4: Putting on the Petals

Take one petal and wrap it around the piece of tape on the top of the straw. That's as easy as it gets. After that, take all the petals and put them on. Just keep wrapping around the layer below. Keep wrapping until all your petals are gone. You're done!

Next, you can put on the stem. Take a long piece of tape and split it in half. Then wrap it around the straw all the way to the end. That is your flower.

Step 5: The Squirter and the Bottle

It's time to make the squirter, the part that will soak your innocent flower sniffer. Take about 3 equal pieces of duct tape and stick them side by side. They must be all flat or else the water will leak. Flatten the tape and then fold it over, equally.

Next, fold the tape in half and tape the bottom. Make it tight or the water will leak. Then do the other side, making it tight. Then do half of the top.

Next, take the water bottle and cut part of the curved piece out. This is the part that will keep the squirter from sticking together. Put the piece back in the squirter. After that you are done with it.

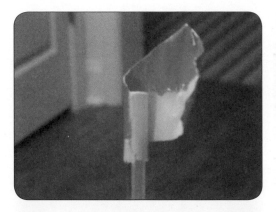

Step 6: Putting the Whole Mess Together

Take the flower and the squirter. Put the flower in the top of the squirter and then put tape on the other side. Secure the whole flower onto the squirter. After that take a bunch of duct tape and wrap it all around the squirter. Make it tight! It will prevent the water from leaking.

When all is said and done, fill it up with water and see if it works. Then spray some perfume on it, and soak away!

Duct Tape Flower Pen

By ashep2020

www.instructables.com/id/
Duct-Tape-Flower-Pen/

Step 1: Gather All Materials

- Duck brand duct tape (any other brand works too)
- Pen (any color works)
- X-Acto Knife (optional, good for clean cuts; scissors also work well)

Step 2: Create the Stem of the Flower

Take your pen and cover it in tape (lengthwise works the best). This step is completed best if you roll the pen across the tape, sticky-side up. Also, if you want a colored center, place a 1-inch piece of tape around the top so it is flat; this way you will have a better-looking flower.

Step 3: Create the Petals of the Flower

To make your petals, cut several strips of 2-inch long duct tape squares.

Step 4: Folding the Petals

Fold one edge over itself sticky side up, leaving some stickiness exposed on the side and bottom.

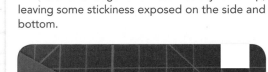

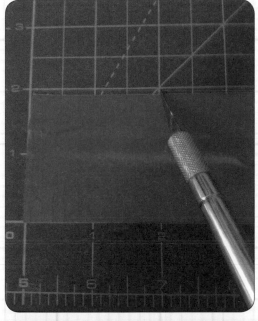

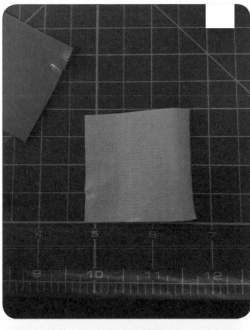

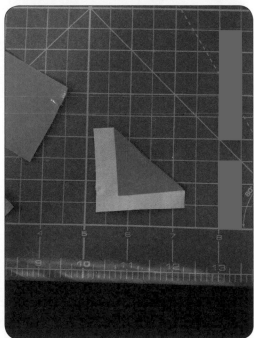

Step 5: Folding the Petals, Continued

Take the other edge and fold it over, leaving only stickiness on the bottom of the strip.

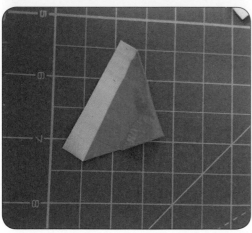

Step 6: Placing the Petals on the Stem

Wrap the petals tightly around the top of the stem.

Step 7: Adding More Petals

Repeat steps 2 to 5 with additional strips of duct tape, wrapping the petals around the top. Continue until you've reached the desired size.

Clothing, Jewelry, and Accessories

100 Percent Authentic Duct Tape Hoodie

By Kaiven

www.instructables.com/id/
100-Authentic-Duct-Tape-Hoodie-
110-yards-of-duc/

I was inspired to make a duct tape jacket of some kind because of hat day at my school. Why hat day, you ask? Well, I didn't have any awesome hats, so I made a hex hat from duct tape. It was a hit with my friends. I was excited to do something bigger. Something with some more "wow" factor.

When first worn, this jacket is kind of stiff and pretty much a plastic tube. It keeps in a LOT of heat, and is great for wearing in the cold outside! It is also 100 percent waterproof, and can be used as a rain jacket. The more you wear it, the more comfortable it gets. Unluckily for me, it is still hot here in the South, even at 5:00 a.m. when I have to go catch the bus for school. Eventually though, I will be wearing this to school every day.

Step 1: Tools and Materials

First, you need the right tools.
- Scissors
- Razor
- Sharpie
- Yardstick

Now, gather your materials.
- Duct tape. I used two 55-yard rolls and part of a 40-yard roll, along with fluorescent green tape for decorating. I probably spent around $15 for the duct tape. I didn't use professional tape—I used the cheapest I could find.
- Masking tape

You also need a large, flat surface that you can cut on. You may wish to use a large cutting board on a table if you need to.

Step 2: Wait—How Big Should It Be?

I must admit—I stole my measurements from imrobot's Instructable at www.instructables.com/id/The-plastic-bag-hoodie-How-to-fuse-plastic-bags-a/#step5. In step 5 he has the measurements. (I've posted it in this step as well.)

Now, be careful! I used the medium measurements for the body, which is 68cm by 61cm. It turns out that this is WAY too wide, and the jacket will be more like a tube. It is best to make the size measurement that is closest to your size, and then tailor the jacket after you finish.

Step 3: Getting Started—Duct Tape Cloth

First, we must learn how to make duct tape cloth!

Making this can be kind of tricky, but mostly just when you are covering the first layer. If 2 sticky parts touch in the wrong place, problems can occur. Be careful when laying down the strips!

There are variations on how to make duct tape cloth, but this method works well for me and lets me get the correct size duct tape sheets I need.

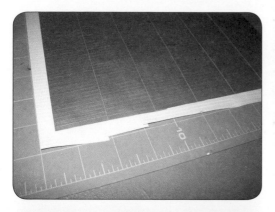

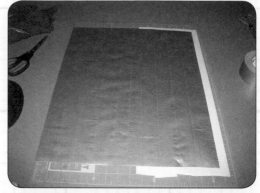

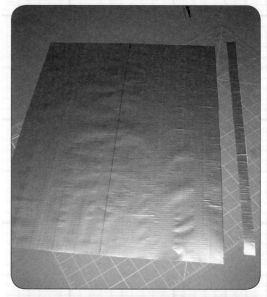

Step 4: Sleeves

We now need to make the sleeves. I started with the sleeves because they are the easiest. Make sure you make a plain rectangle the correct width. (Mine was 24cm by 39cm by 55cm. Fifty-five centimeters was a tad short for me—adjust to your size.)

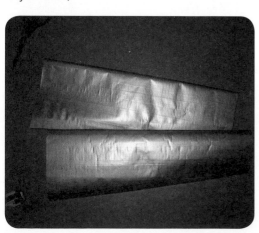

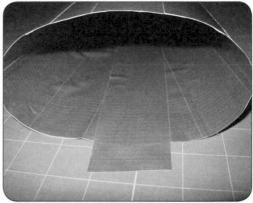

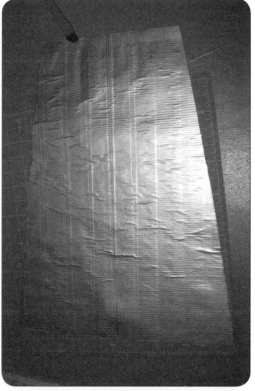

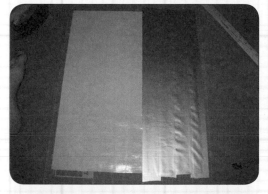

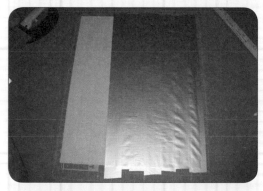

Step 5: Starting the Body

The main body is large. So large, in fact, that it did not fit on my cutting board. I used my floor to make the body and, using masking tape, a yardstick, and a Sharpie, made a large measuring angle to get the correct size duct tape cloth.

If you want a zipper or a cut down the middle, make sure to measure and mark off the middle of one of the duct tape sheets.

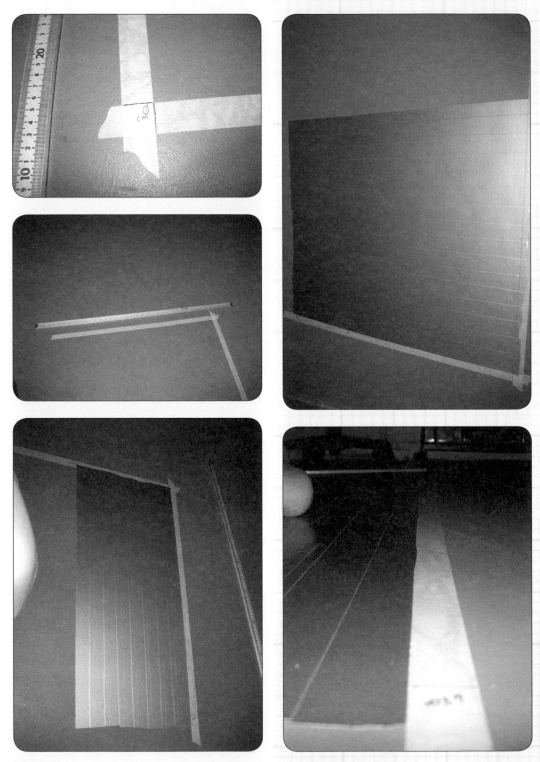

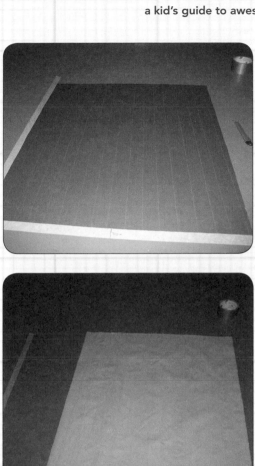

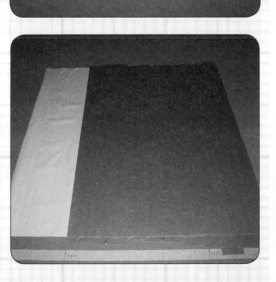

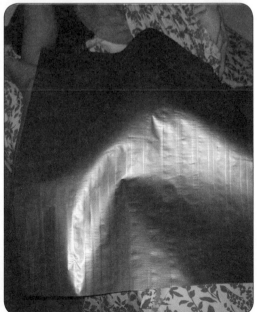

Step 6: Attaching Things

We begin the end of the hoodie. The easiest way to go about attaching the pieces is to first attach the 2 halves, then the sleeves, then the sides of the body. There could be another way, but I didn't see how I was going to get duct tape strips into the enclosed area of the hoodie.

The hardest part of this step is adding duct tape to the inside seam of the sleeves. It is dark inside a plastic tunnel.

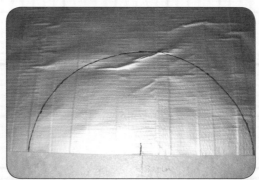

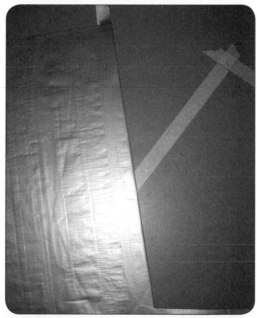

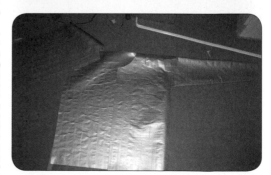

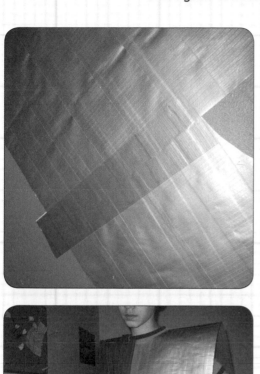

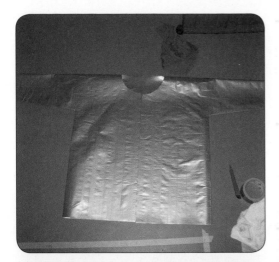

Step 7: Tailoring and Pockets!

I decided to tailor the jacket and make it fit better. I also decided to work on some pockets, because they are easy!

Note: After using the jacket, the pockets are less than impractical. They are designed too tightly, and my hands barely fit, let alone any objects.

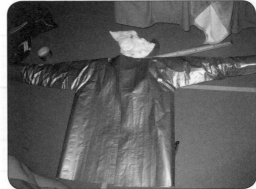

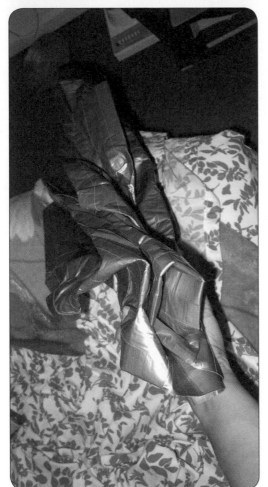

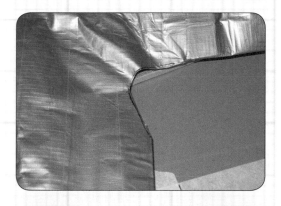

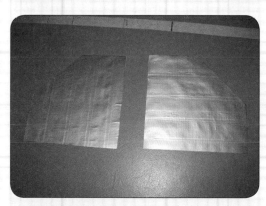

Step 8: The Long-Awaited Hood

Making the hood is pretty straightforward. All you need to do is join the 2 rectangles and attach them to the collar of the hoodie. Trim off the top corner of the hood and round it to make it look nicer.

29

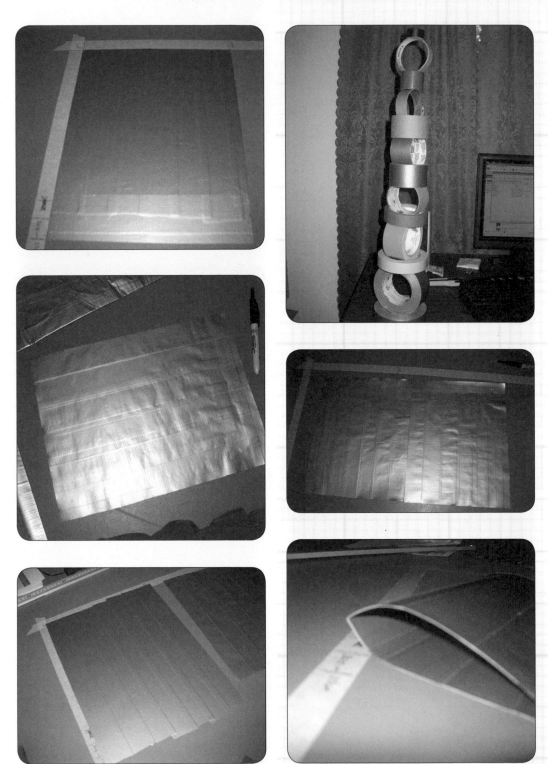

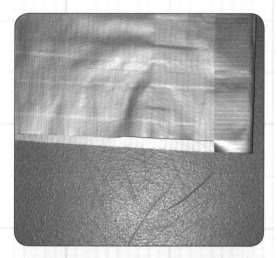

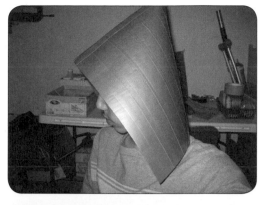

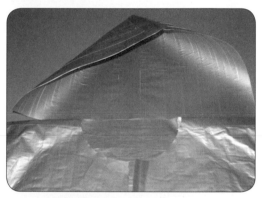

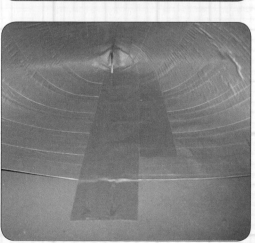

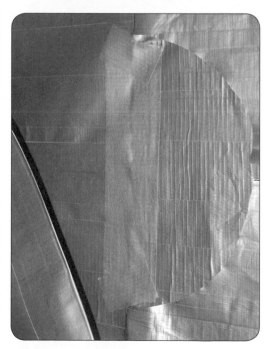

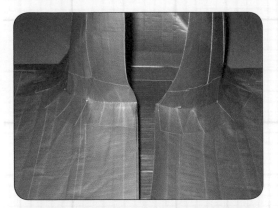

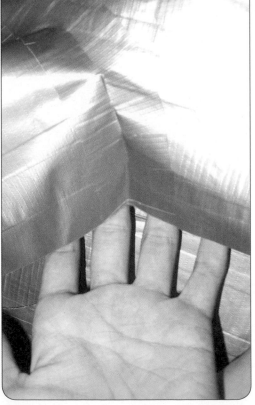

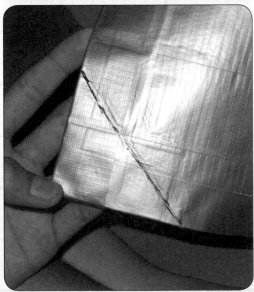

Step 9: Finishing Up!

The hoodie is technically done. But there's nothing like some colored duct tape to make it look snazzy. You can put on a bunch of stripes, checkered squares, or pictures and words with colored duct tape. I just did an easy choice and put one color of duct tape on what I consider to be the borders of the jacket.

After 5 days of work, I finished!

Don't be fooled—it takes a while, but it really isn't hard. This jacket holds in a *lot* of heat. I mean, while taking the pictures for this in my air-conditioned room, I started sweating. It is pretty comfortable if it is cool outside with less sun.

This jacket is also 100 percent waterproof! So it's a bonus if it rains while you are outside in the cold. I tested this with a garden hose, and it repels water very efficiently. The biggest issue is that the water drips directly onto your pants. Maybe future developments will fix this.

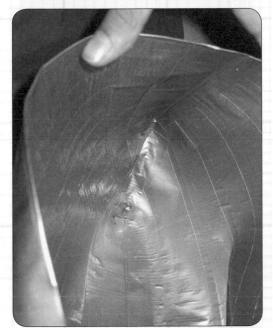

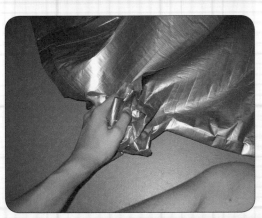

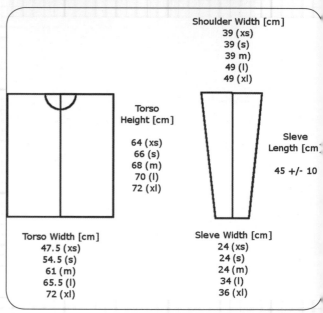

Shoulder Width [cm]
39 (xs)
39 (s)
39 m)
49 (l)
49 (xl)

Torso
Height [cm]

64 (xs)
66 (s)
68 (m)
70 (l)
72 (xl)

Sleve
Length [cm]

45 +/- 10

Torso Width [cm]
47.5 (xs)
54.5 (s)
61 (m)
65.5 (l)
72 (xl)

Sleve Width [cm]
24 (xs)
24 (s)
24 (m)
34 (l)
36 (xl)

Duct Tape Flip Flops

By watermelonhead
www.instructables.com/id/
Duct-Tape-Flip-Flops/

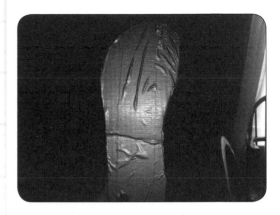

Flip flops are fun and easy to wear, and even more so when made out of duct tape! All you'll need is duct tape, a pair of flip flops, scissors, a pen, and a template of your flip flop. To make the template just trace your flip flops on some cardboard and cut the shapes out. For this project, it would look a lot prettier if I had used colored duct tape, but I lost my purple duct tape and I'm too lazy to buy more.

Step 1: Lots of Duct Tape

Cover one template with duct tape, front and back. Don't skimp on this, unless you want crappy flip flops! It should look like a big rectangle. Then trim the edges so it actually looks like a shoe again. Step on this with the right (correct) foot and mark the spot in between your big toe and the one next to it with the pen.

Step 2: The Tab Thingy

Warning: This part can be tricky if you don't look at the pictures. Look at them! Measure the height of your big toe and add ¼ inch to that height. Then multiply that number by 4. Cut a half strip of duct tape that length. Then make a tab with it—see the first picture. Line up the fold on the bottom with the mark you made in the previous step and tape it to the base. Try it on to see if it's comfortable.

Making the straps is a very inaccurate process. Make a strip out of duct tape by folding a long piece of duct tape in half. Then, put your foot on the shoe pad with the tab between your toes and tape the strip to the tab, curve it over your foot, and tape it to the bottom of the pad. Then cut a half strip of duct tape and secure the inside of the strap with the pad (see picture). Repeat with the other strap. Then place a half strip of duct tape over the "valley" made by the 2 straps (see the picture).

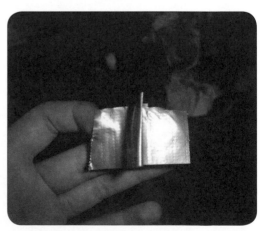

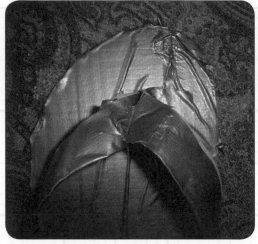

Step 3: Repeat and Decorate!

Repeat with the other flip flop! Easy. Then you can decorate with anything you want—ribbon, yarn, other duct tape, etc. I didn't want to decorate with anything, myself.

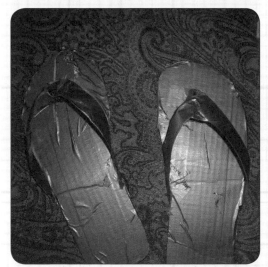

Bow Ring out of Duct Tape

By hdaniellet

www.instructables.com/id/
Bow-Ring-Out-Of-Duct-Tape/

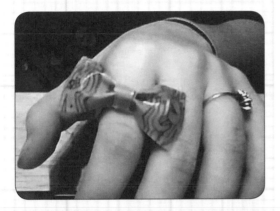

Step 1: You Will Need
- A bit of duct tape
- A ruler or similar object for measuring
- Scissors/X-Acto knife/sharp-edged thing

Step 2: Cut Tape
Cut yourself a decent length of duct tape (about 3 inches), then clip the ends just a bit so it looks clean and even. Measure your clean strip 2 inches from one end, then SNIP!

Step 3: Decorate
Doodle (if you want) on your 2-inch strip.

Step 4: Scrunch
Turn your strip over, if you doodled, to the plain side. Scrunch a little of the top to the inside then pinch it to the middle. Do the same to the bottom.

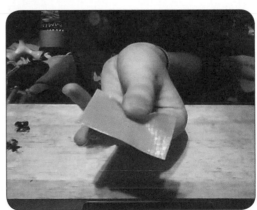

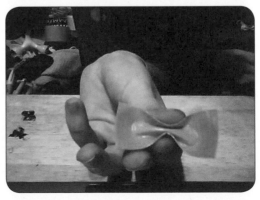

Step 5: Secure Scrunch

Cut a slim strip, the length of the width of the duct tape, and wrap it around the middle of the bow to keep it scrunched.

Step 6: Create Band

Now cut a 4-inch strip of duct tape about ½ inch in width. Fold it in half; this will be the band.

Step 7: Attach Band

Align the middle of the bow to the middle of the band and tape them together with a skinny strip of tape the length of the width of duct tape.

Step 8: Put It On!

Put the band on your finger bow side up. Size the flaps to your finger and mark where they end. Tape them down with a tiny piece of tape.

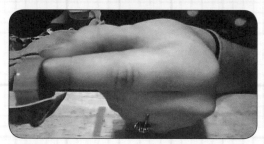

Step 9: Final Step

Check durability, fix mistakes, spruce it up, and you're done!

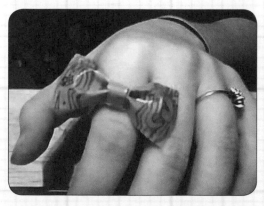

Girly Duct Tape Wallet/Clutch

By jerseygirl77
www.instructables.com/id/Girly-duct-
tape-walletclutch/

All of the duct tape wallets I've seen so far look like they belong in the pockets of overalls or inside a tool box. This one is a lot more feminine. It won't really fit in a pants pocket, but it is a great, sturdy, everyday wallet with room for 8 cards, and it is big enough that you could carry it separately as a clutch.

Step 1: What You Will Need

- Lots of duct tape
- Scissors
- Nail polish remover and toilet paper to clean the gunk off the scissors
- Pen/marker
- A straight edge

Step 2: Make the Base

At the base of this wallet are 2 sheets of duct tape. I've found that the easiest way to make one of these sheets is to start with a piece of loose leaf and cover that in duct tape on both sides. That way you can get nice straight lines. It also adds a bit more stability.

One of the base sheets should be 10 inches x 9½ inches and should be folded into 3 sections. The first is for the cards, the second is the pocket for the money, and the third is the flap with the Velcro. You can see these on the finished wallet. Once you make it, fold it to the appropriate proportions. The 2 larger sections should be about 4 inches long.

The second sheet should be 4 inches x 9½ inches. This one is taped in the middle and is part of the pocket for the money.

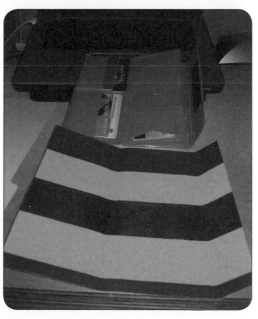

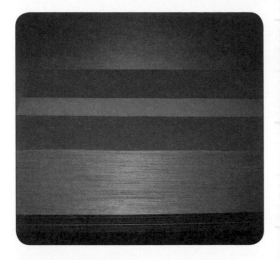

Step 3: Tape the Base Together

Make 1 strip of duct tape either by using the loose leaf or just by lining 2 strips up together. Cut 2 lengths about 3 to 3½ inches long. Fold them in half lengthwise and then cut them into triangles (see the picture). Then tape these to the short sides of the smaller sheet. Then tape the long side of that small sheet to the large sheet at the fold between the 2 larger sections.

Then, finally, tape the free sides of the triangles (in orange) to the middle section of the big sheet so that you get a pocket big enough for money.

This sounds confusing but I think the pictures make it relatively clear.

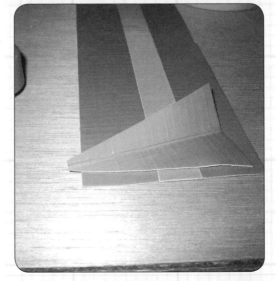

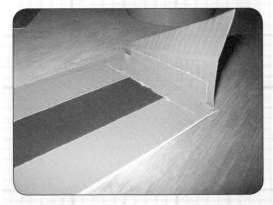

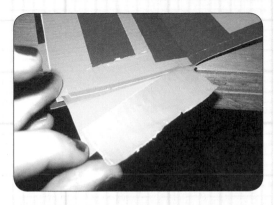

Step 4: The Card Slots

The wallet holds 8 cards, but I do 2 per slot, so there are only 4 slots.

1. Take 2 cards and wrap them lengthwise with duct tape, sticky side out.
2. Slide the little sleeve you made down so that a reasonable amount of the card is showing (so that you would be able to grab card).
3. Make cuts on each end of the duct tape that is now sticking out over the sides. Then fold those down.
4. Slide the sleeve down again so that the folds are at the top of what will be the card pocket.
5. Take another piece of duct tape and put it over the bottom of the card pocket (sticky part out).
6. Then put that on one side of the bottom section of the big sheet, towards the top (see picture).
7. Repeat steps 1 through 6, except put it on the other side.
8. Next, lay a piece of tape over those 2 pockets so that the sticky part is covered.
9. Repeat the whole thing to make another row of pockets on the bottom.

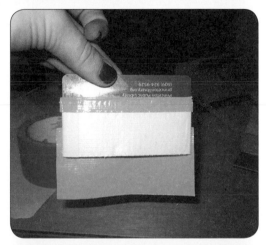

Step 5: The Finishing Touches

Add some strips or half strips to all of the exposed sides and joints just to make it sturdy and a bit prettier. Then fold it all up and add some Velcro to the top, the smallest section, and the front flap. I didn't have any Velcro on hand for this wallet, but I included a picture of an old one to show the placement.

Now you've got a nice big wallet with room for plenty of cash and 8 cards.

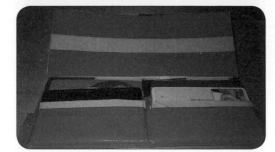

Duct Tape Bows

By skipro

www.instructables.com/id/
Duct-Tape-Bows/

Duct tape bows are great—you can put them on shoes, clips, or bracelets!

Step 1: Pick Your Colors

First, take either 1 or 2 colors—2 colors if you want each side of the bow to be different. Take your color and eye how big you want your piece to be. Normally I do 1½ by 1½ inches. Fold over the piece of duct tape while it is still attached to the roll. Rip or cut the duct tape where the sticky and non-sticky sides meet so you have a square that is not sticky. Make one identical in size in the other color.

Step 2: Fold the Tape

Before you start this step, rip a piece of duct tape ½ inch wide. You will need it later. Then, take one of the squares and fold a sixth of the square towards the other end. Then, without letting go, flip the whole piece over so the non-folded part of the square is toward you, and then bring the folded side up and crease so it is the same size as your last fold. Flip and fold, flip and fold, until there's nothing left and you have tape that looks like an accordion. Do the same with the other square.

Step 3:

Take 5 duct tape rolls and stack them. If you don't have enough duct tape, you can use 5 practical things that weigh about the same as 5 duct tape rolls would. Take your folded squares and put them underneath the rolls. I know it sounds silly, but it works! Leave them there for about 2 minutes and then take them out.

Step 4: The Final Step!

After you take them out, use the strip of duct tape you ripped before to tape the squares together.

Step 5: Done!
Enjoy!

Woven Duct Tape Bracelet

By DuctTapeCrazy

www.instructables.com/id/Woven-Duct-Tape-Bracelet/

This is an Instructable on how to make a stylish duct tape bracelet for men or women. The bracelet is very durable and it is also waterproof.

Step 1: Tools and Materials

- Scissors or craft knife
- 3 colors of duct tape

Step 2: The Strips

You want to make 3 strips that are about 4 inches long and ⅖ inch wide.

Fold down a strip to ⅖ inch at the top, and then keep folding it down. Do this to all 3 strips. Trim the ends of these pieces.

Step 3: The Weaving

The weaving is the hardest part, but it only takes 5 minutes.

1. Determine what color you want to be the center (inside). You can put the other colors in any order.
2. Use a strip of tape to hold the strips together at the top.
3. Weave the tape (use the diagram).
4. Done! Now tape the ends together and you have a bracelet.

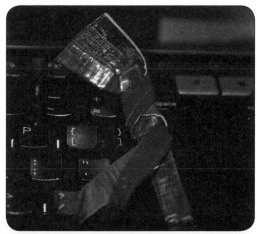

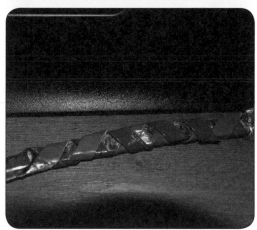

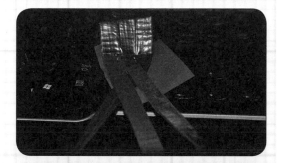

Step 1: Things You Will Need

- Scissors
- Duct tape (1 or 2 rolls, if you want different colors)
- A duct tape bow (optional)

Step 2: Making the Structure

First, cut your duct tape into 6 strips, each 10 inches lengthwise. It's ok if they're not perfect; you can just cut the sides that are messed up off. Then, with the sticky side up, you take all 6 strips of duct tape and stick them together by slightly overlapping the edges (as shown in the picture).

Step 3: Making the Base

Once you have all your rectangles overlapping each other and stuck together, get more 10-inch lengths and put them on top of the ones you just made, this time with the "pretty" side up (a.k.a., put them together sticky side to sticky side). Cut off all ends if necessary to make it even with the other sides.

Step 4: The Folding Begins

Take your duct tape and fold it in half (hamburger-style) and crease it till you have it perfectly secure.

Step 5: Putting the Sides On

Take a strip of duct tape about 3 inches long and tear it in half (if you want to). Use these pieces to close off the ends of your coin purse (the folded duct tape "hamburger") so that the only opening is at the top. (If you're confused, just look at the pictures.)

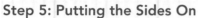

Step 6: Bring the Bows

This part is optional, but if you totally adore bows like me, this is perfect for your coin holder. Take a bow that you already have made and place it where you want it to be on your coin holder. Next, you will just take the bow and run some duct tape over the very middle.

Step 7: How to Make the Bow for Step 6

Take a piece of duct tape (about 3 inches long) and put another strip on top, sticky side to sticky side. Fold into 4 sections, as if you are making a fan or accordion. Take a little strip of duct tape and then attach to it so it holds it in place!

47

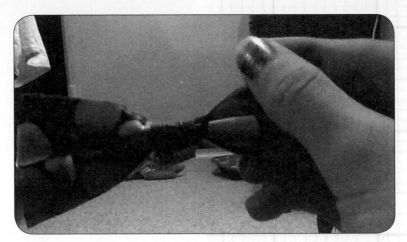

How to Make Duct Tape Feather Earrings

By socksmonkeysduckstape
www.instructables.com/id/How-To-Make-Duct-Tape-Feather-Earrings/

Step 1: Tools and Materials
- Earring hooks from a craft kit or old dangly earrings
- Wire (two 6-inch pieces)
- Scissors (I have my goopy, sticky duct tape ones and my clean ones)
- Duct tape

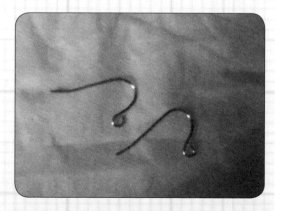

Step 2: Attaching the Wire to the Earrings

Fold the wire in half so the tips are meeting. Put your earring hook onto the halfway mark and twist. If you need to, use pliers to help twist the wire to the end. The twists do not need to be very tight, but tight enough so the earring will not slip off of it. You can trim the wire depending on how long you want your earrings. The wire will go all the way down your earring, so however long your wire is, that's how long your earrings are.

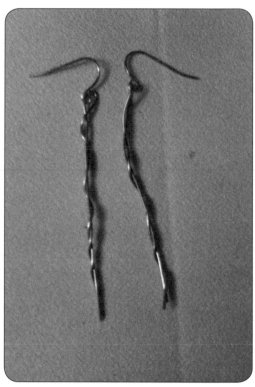

Step 3: Making Your Feather and Putting It onto the Wire

Cut or rip a piece of duct tape as long as you want; this will be the length of your feather. Attach the sticky side of your piece and put it onto the top of the wire. Cut another piece the same length and put the 2 pieces on top of each other, making a piece of duct tape fabric on your wire. Make slits and cuts in the duct tape fabric to make it look like a feather. For the other earring, you can put your first finished one over the second and trace it! Then they will look the same. I ended up making my feathers longer than the wire, but you can do it either way.

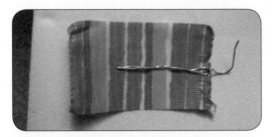

Step 4: Show off Your New Earrings!

Make more and show them off! You made them, so have fun.

Step 5: Clean Up Your Work Area

Clean, clean, clean! Then you have more space for creating more cool things.

Duct tape is used for pretty much everything. Make a cute headband with just duct tape and scissors.

Step 1: The Bow

Cut a piece of duct tape about 16 inches long. Fold it in half.

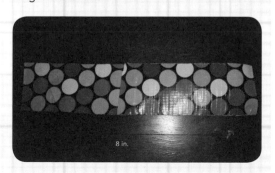

Step 2: Fold Again

Fold it in half again. Cut a small piece of duct tape about ½ inch long. Tape the ends together.

Step 3: Shape Bow

Move the bow so the piece of tape added in step 2 is in the middle. Fold the middle of the bow to shape it.

Step 4: The Headband, Part 1

Cut a ½-inch piece of the duct tape for the headband part. Wrap the tape around the middle to hold it together. Cut a piece of duct tape long enough to go around your head. Fold it in half. Trim the edge.

Step 5: Add the Bow

Cut a ½-inch piece of duct tape. Tape the bow to the middle of the headband. Tape the ends of the headband together.

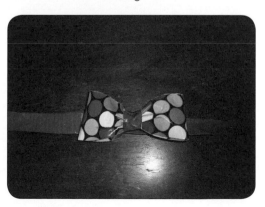

Woven Duct Tape Clutch

By socksmonkeysduckstape
www.instructables.com/id/Woven-Duct-tape-Clutch/

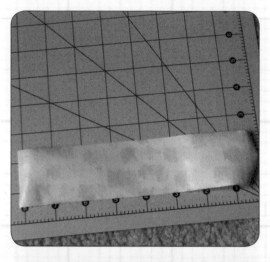

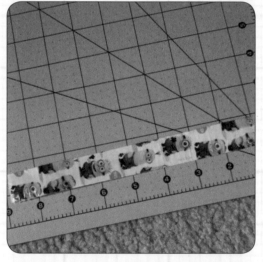

Step 1: Create Strips for the Weave

Make four 9-inch strips and fold them in half. Then make eight 4-inch strips and fold them over just like the others. Trim if needed.

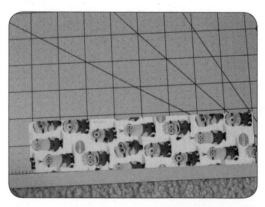

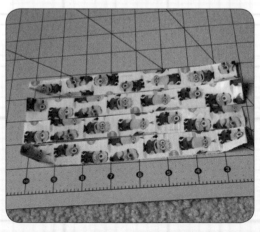

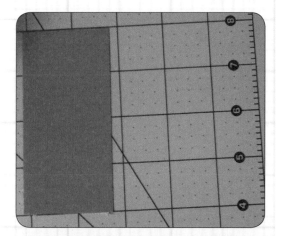

Step 2: Weave

Weave the strips. Tape them down to your workplace and, when weaved, fold other strips backward.

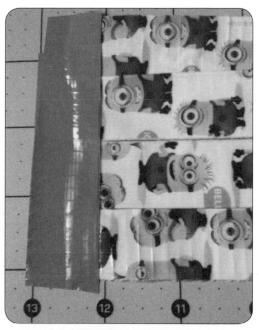

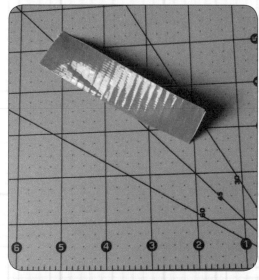

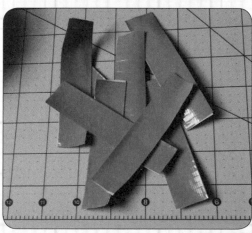

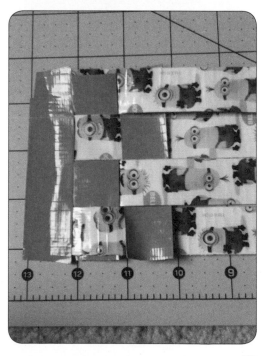

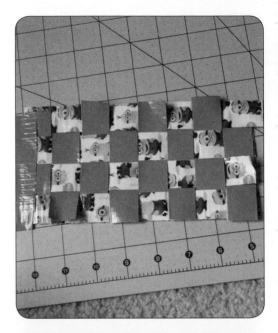

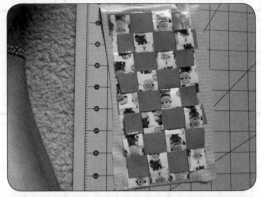

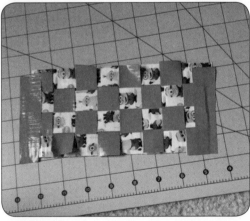

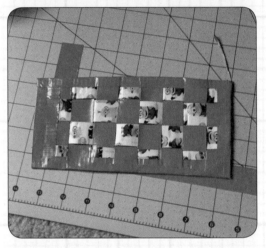

Step 3: Make the Back

Make a back out of three 9-inch strips overlapped. Flip it over and put two 9-inch strips on it. Fold the top halfway.

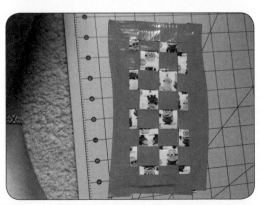

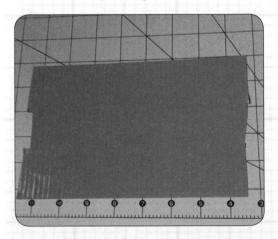

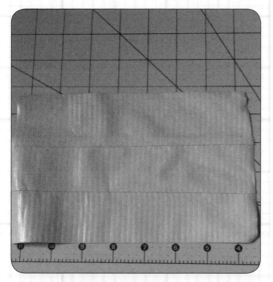

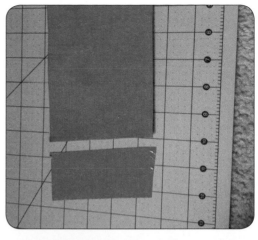

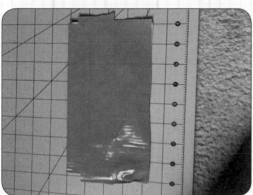

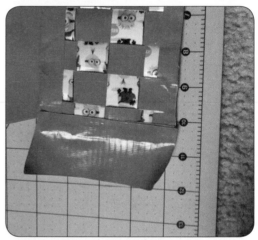

Step 4: Connect the Back

Use little pieces of tape to connect the back to the front.

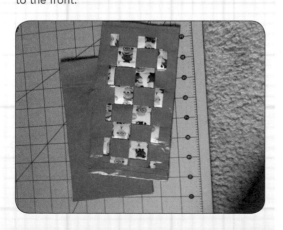

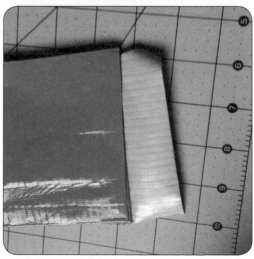

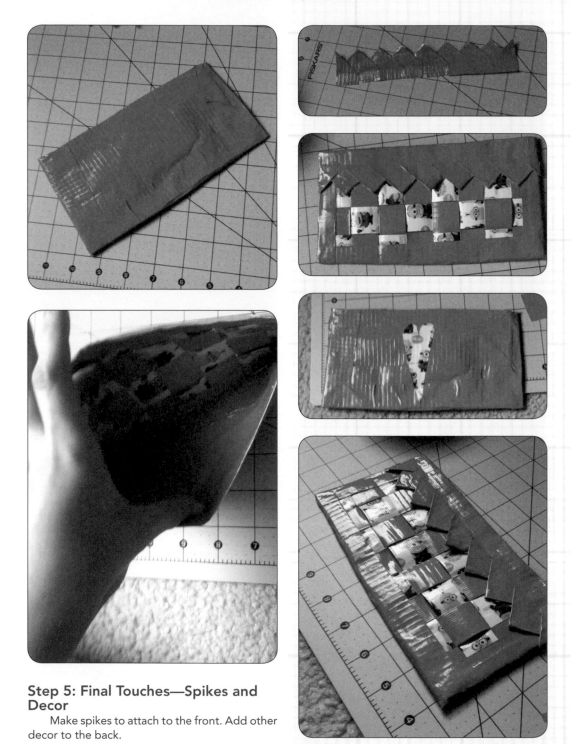

Step 5: Final Touches—Spikes and Decor

Make spikes to attach to the front. Add other decor to the back.

How to Make a Spiked Duct Tape Bracelet

By socksmonkeysduckstape
www.instructables.com/id/How-To-Make-A-Spiked-Duck-Tape-Bracelet/

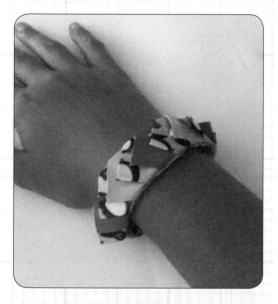

Step 1: What You'll Need

Duct tape! You'll want 2 or 3 colors to make a pattern or just 1 if you want a monochromatic look.

Step 2: Make the Spike

Take a little piece of duct tape that is approximately 2 inches long. Fold over one corner to the middle, then the other. Stick it on your workplace.

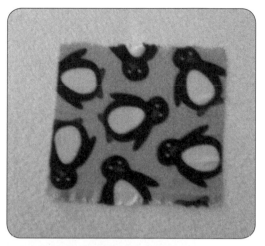

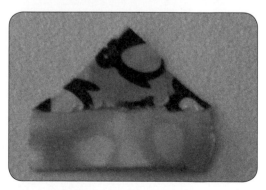

Step 3: Make More Spikes

Depending on the age of the maker, make the following number of spikes: for ages 1 to 4 make 13; for ages 5 to 7 make 15; for ages 8 to 12 make 18; for ages 13 to 18 make 20; and for 19+ make 21 to 22. Attach them to the previous petal—this is important! Make sure all of the petals are touching the one before it! Otherwise it will all fall apart.

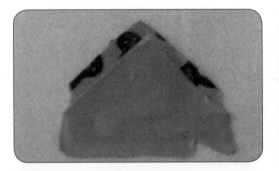

Step 5: Folding

Turn it over so it's sticky side up. Fold one side to the middle, and then the other side, so they line up in the middle. Put a strip of tape over the back.

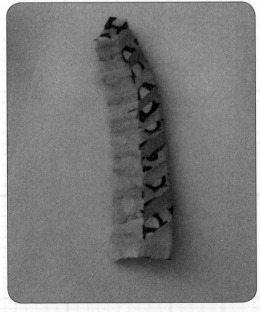

Step 4: Peel

Peel the long strand of spikes off of your workspace. If it breaks, put a skinny piece of duct tape on the bottom of the last one and attach again.

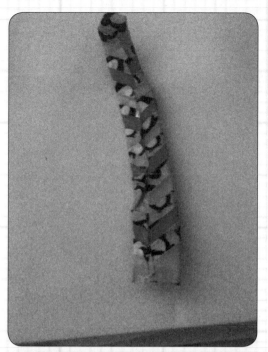

Step 6: Turn It Over and Wear!

Make a tiny, skinny strip to attach it. You can use Velcro or a magnet, too. Wear it and rock it!

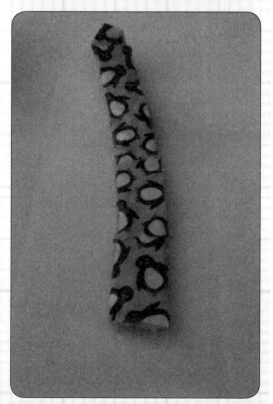

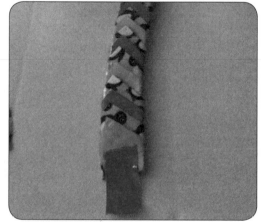

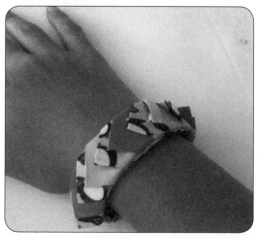

How to Make a Duct Tape Hair Bow

By superdes1

www.instructables.com/id/
How-to-Make-a-Duct-Tape-Hair-Bow/

Let's make a duct tape hair bow!

Step 1: Tools and Materials

- Your favorite color of duct tape
- Bobby pin
- Ruler
- Scissors or an X-Acto knife

Step 2: Cut Tape

Cut an 18½-inch piece of duct tape.

Step 3: Fold Tape

Fold the piece in half, but leave a little piece of sticky side still free. Then curve it like you are making a bracelet.

Step 4: More Folding

Fold the top in half towards you and then push the sides down. Do the same with the bottom half. Cut a small piece of tape and wrap it around the middle.

Step 5: Bobby Pin

Take another small piece and wrap it around the top half of the bobby pin.

Step 6: Wear It

Open the bobby pin up and wear it in your hair!

Thin Duct Tape Wallet

By MartinMakes
www.instructables.com/id/
Thin-Duct-Tape-Wallet/

This is my contribution to the many duct tape wallets out there. I was inspired by some of the minimalist wallets online and at www.everyday-carry.com.

This wallet is very simple to make and looks great when you use 2 different tape colors, as you can see. It has a section for bills and 2 pockets on either side for cards.

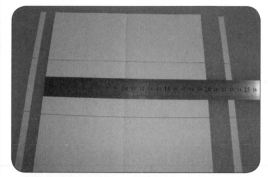

Step 1: Make the Paper Template

1. Divide the paper into 3. I used 7 cm for each section. Cut off the excess.
2. Fold the paper in half to get the midline.
3. Measure 10 cm from the midline to either side and cut off the excess.
4. Use the inside of a duct tape roll and mark an arc in the center segment on the midline.
5. Make folds on the segment lines.
   Now you are ready for the duct tape.

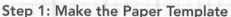

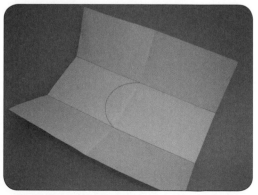

Step 2: Make the Inside of the Wallet

1. Stick a length of tape in the center of the paper. You need to start here so that your overlaps are in the correct direction. If not, bills you put into the wallet will snag on the overlap as you put them in.
2. Use a ruler as a gauge for the overlap size.
3. With the ruler in place, stick a length of tape onto the paper with the overlap on top of the first tape.
4. Repeat step 3 to cover the paper, making sure you have some overhang at the top and bottom of the paper.
5. Turn the paper over and trim off the excess on the sides. Fold the overhang onto the paper.
6. Fold the paper in half at the midline and cut out the arc with scissors.
7. Unfold and smooth out.
8. Fold the segments in, to overlap each other, to create a good crease.
9. Now fold in half at the midline to create a crease.

    You are now ready to add the outside tape.

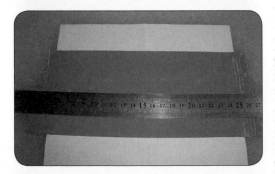

6. Repeat step 5 for the other side.
7. Fold the wallet in half and smooth out the creases. Your wallet is done.

    I put the wallet under some heavy books for some time to flatten it out.

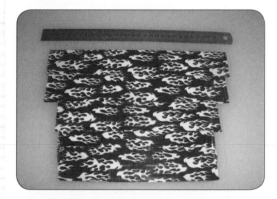

Step 3: Make the Outside of the Wallet

1. Stick a length of tape at the top of the paper a small way down from the edge. This will give the wallet a nice look when it is complete. Make sure you have a lot of overhang on the sides. You will use this to stick the wallet together; you only need to do this for the length of the first segment.
2. Use the overlap method form step 3 of "Make the Inside."
3. Continue this to the bottom of the paper. With the last length of tape, start at the bottom and overlap to the top.
4. Turn it over. Trim off the excess from after the first segment. Fold it in half, cut out the hole, and then unfold.
5. Fold the wallet with the inside overlapping in. Square up the ends and fold the first segment overhang over the folded wallet side to stick it down.

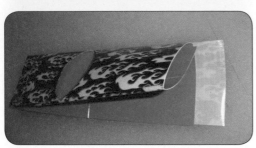

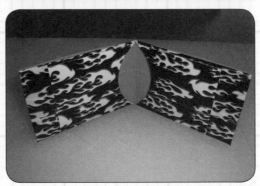

64

Woven Duct Tape Bag

By theimpossiblegirl_1
www.instructables.com/id/Woven-Duct-Tape-Bag/

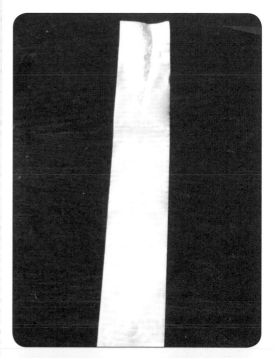

I was inspired by doormatyay's duct tape tote post but used a completely different method from hers.

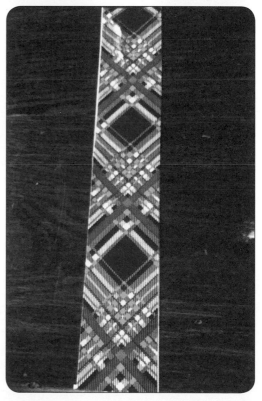

Step 1: Create First Set of Strips

Cut out a piece of duct tape that is 1 foot long and lay it sticky side up. Then cut out another piece of duct tape that is also 1 foot long and place the sticky side onto the sticky side of the other piece of duct tape. You have created 1 strip. Continue this until you have 6 strips.

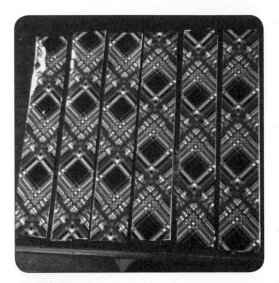

Step 2: Create Second Set of Strips

Repeat first step, but this time with a different color.

Step 3: Fix Strips

Cut all strips so that they measure 11½ inches. If necessary, cut off excess sticky parts from the sides of the strips.

Step 4: Weave First Strip

Lay out all strips from step 2 horizontally. Take 1 strip from step 1 and place it on top of the first strip, then under the second strip, then on top of the third strip, etc., until you have woven it through all of the strips from step 2.

Step 5: Duct Tape End 1

Take a different color from steps 1 and 2 and use it to duct tape the ends together. Next, carefully lift up all duct tape pieces and flip to the other side, then cut off the excess duct tape on the ends. Lift sticky side of duct tape and press it onto the tips of the duct tape strips.

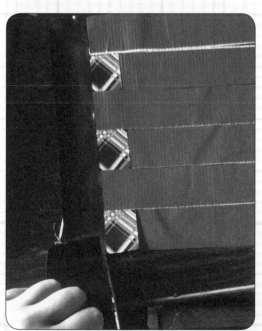

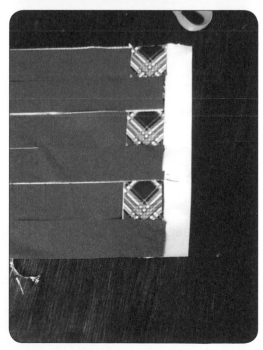

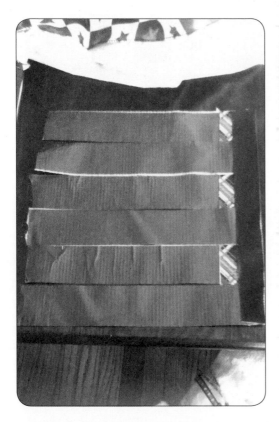

Step 7: Duct Tape End 2
Repeat step 5.

Step 6: Weave Second Strip
Repeat step 4, this time on other end.

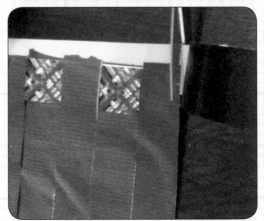

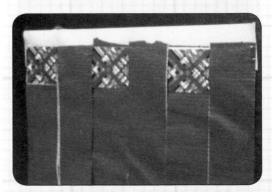

Step 8: Weave Remaining Pieces

Use the same under-over method from previous steps until all strips are woven.

Step 9: Duct Tape Side 1

This is the same as steps 5 and 7.

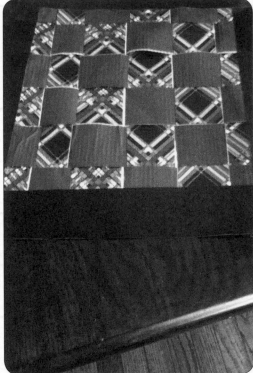

Step 10: Duct Tape Side 2

Repeat step 9.

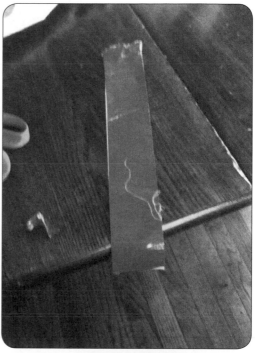

Step 11: Create Second Side

Repeat ALL steps once so that you have 2 identical sheets of woven duct tape.

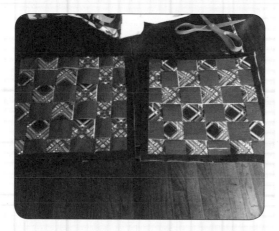

Step 12: Create Bottom for Bag

Repeat step 1 (make sure strip is 11½ inches though) to make the flat bottom of the bag, then measure 11½ inches and cut out a one-sided strip of duct tape. Rip that piece in half. Take one of the one-sided strips and tape it to one of the long-sided ends of the 2-sided strip. Do the same with the other one-sided strip. After that is finished, take one of the sheets of woven duct tape and attach it to one of the sides of the double-sided duct tape, then repeat with the other side.

Step 13: Create Sides
Repeat previous step twice.

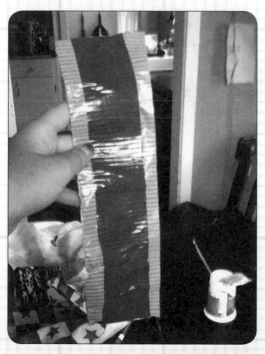

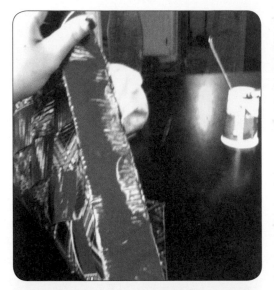

Step 14: Create Strap

Cut out a long strip of duct tape, wrap it over your arm to measure to liking, then cut the strip and make sure it is one-sided. Fold the sheet into thirds, then cut out a piece of one-sided duct tape (preferably short length, but any measurement will do) and use it to tape one of the tips of the strap to one of the sides of the bag. Repeat. Good job.

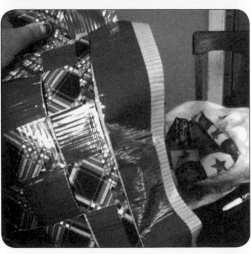

Hats

How to Make a Duct Tape Hat

By macananadado
www.instructables.com/id/
How-to-make-a-duct-tape-hat-1/

In this project you will learn how to make a duct tape flat-bill hat.

Step 1: Tools and Materials

- Pencil
- X-Acto knife
- Ruler
- Marker
- Cutting board
- Construction paper

Step 2: Measure

Draw a line that is 10 cm long, and then mark the center of the line. Make a mark on that center line that is 16½ cm high, then make a mark 9½ cm high. From that 9½ cm mark draw a line 4 cm out from both sides.

Step 3: Duct Tape

Lay down pieces of duct tape long enough to fit the template, then trace the template onto the non-sticky side of the duct tape. Cut the shape out with the X-Acto knife. Flip it over and cover that side with duct tape, then trim off the extra tape. Repeat this process 5 more times so that you are left with 6 pieces.

Step 4: Connect Tape Triangles

Cut pieces 9½ cm of duct tape, then cut them in half lengthwise. You will use these to connect the triangle-shaped pieces. Stick them on half of the triangle pieces, then stick another triangle piece on the sticky part still exposed, making sure to leave a little space between the triangles. Then put the other piece of duct tape on top of the sticky side of the piece that you just laid down. Repeat the process with all the triangles, and then connect the ends so it makes a ring.

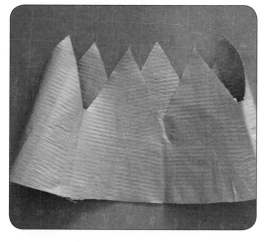

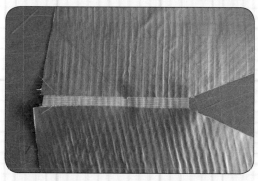

Step 5: Close up Top of Hat

Flip hat over with little flaps facing down, closing off the crown of the hat. Cut 3-inch pieces into thirds and apply them to the inside of the hat. Then flip it over and do the same to the outside.

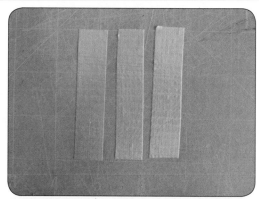

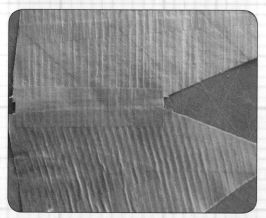

Step 6: Reinforce the Brim

Take a piece of construction paper and cut pieces that are 2 inches wide and as long as the paper length. Fold them into thirds, then get a strip of duct tape that is a little bit longer than the paper, lay down the paper, and cut slits in the duct tape so when you put it in the hat it doesn't crumple. Put the paper/tape on the inside of the hat along the rim. Repeat 3 times all around the rim.

Step 7: Making the Bill

Take a piece of cardboard and trace out the outline of the bill of the hat. Cover the whole thing in the color of duct tape that you want. Then take 1-inch strips and put them on the top of the bill that touches the hat. Cut slits into the 1-inch strips and pull them up, but not off, and put the bill onto the hat. Do the same to the bottom.

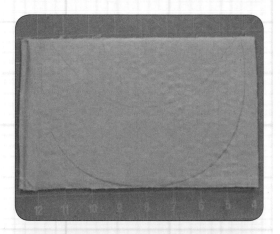

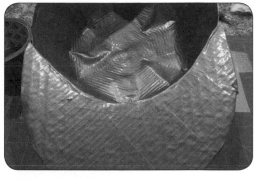

Step 8: Finished
You are done!

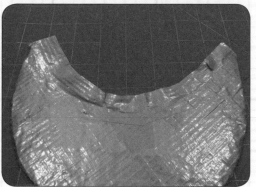

Duct Tape Pirate Hat

By bejbej

**www.instructables.com/id/
Duct-Tape-Pirate-Hat/**

Scallywags! It's time to set sail in search of booty. But every pirate be needin' a faithful hat. And I got just the instructions for you.

Step 1: Materials and Tools

It will take approximately 2 hours to finish the duct tape pirate hat.

Materials:

- 2 rolls of black duct tape
- 1 roll of gray duct tape

Tools:

- Door frame at least 18 inches wide
- A head-sized and head-shaped object to build the crown around
- Marker or pen
- Ruler
- Knife or scissors

Step 2: Brim

Find a door frame that is at least 18 inches wide. (Any frame at least 18 inches wide will work.) This will be used to form the brim of the hat.

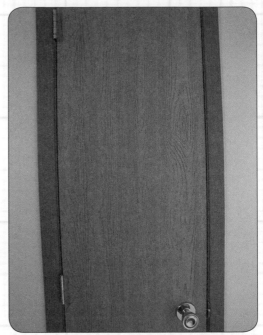

Step 3: Start Duct Tape

Add a strip of silver duct tape horizontally across the frame. The tape shouldn't leave a residue if you work quickly. If you are worried, you can put painter's tape on the door frame first.

Step 4: More Tape

Add another strip of silver duct tape across the frame below the first strip. Overlap the strips by ¼ inch.

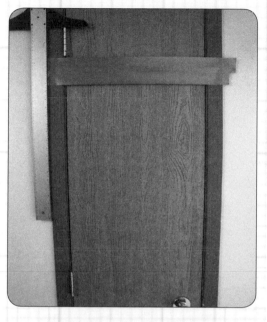

Step 5: Add Strips

Continue adding strips until you have at least an 18-inch by 18-inch square of duct tape.

Step 6: Vertical Strips

Start adding strips of duct tape vertically across the horizontal strips.

Step 7: More Strips

Continue adding vertical strips of duct tape until you have at least an 18-inch by 18-inch square of duct tape that is 2 layers of duct tape thick.

Step 8: Layers

Continue adding layers of duct tape until you have at least an 18-inch by 18-inch square of duct tape that is 4 layers of duct tape thick.

Step 9: Final Layer

Add a final layer of black duct tape.

Step 10: Remove Sheet

Carefully remove the 5-layer sheet of duct tape and lay it down on a table with the sticky side up.

Step 11: Add Black

Add a layer of black duct tape to the sticky side. BE VERY CAREFUL. If the sticky sides of 2 duct tape strips come into contact, they will be almost impossible to separate.

Step 12: Result

You should have a sheet of duct tape 6 layers thick that is black on both sides.

Step 13: Draw Circle

Draw a circle with a diameter of 18 inches in the center of the black sheet of duct tape.

Step 14: Cut Circle

Use a knife or scissors to cut out the circle. Discard the outside scrap. It is no longer needed. Set aside the black duct tape circle.

Step 15: Find a Hat Form

Find something roughly head-shaped and head-sized. I used 2 bowls. Make sure whatever you use is larger than your head, or the hat will not fit. This will be used to form the crown of the hat.

Step 16: Wrap Tape

Wrap duct tape around the outside of the bowl with the sticky side facing outwards. Make sure the bowl is entirely covered. This is the most awkward and hardest part of these instructions.

Step 17: Add Black

Add bits of black duct tape until there are no more exposed sticky sides.

Step 18: Cut Stray Bits

Cut off any dangling bits of black duct tape.

Step 19: Mark Circle

Use the crown to mark a circle on the black duct tape circle.

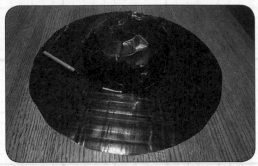

Step 20: Cut Circle

Use a knife or scissors to cut out the smaller circle. The black duct tape circle should now be the correct shape to become the hat's brim. Discard the smaller black duct tape circle. It is no longer needed.

Step 21: Align

Align the crown with the hole in the center of the brim.

Step 22: Attach

Use small pieces of duct tape to attach the crown to the brim.

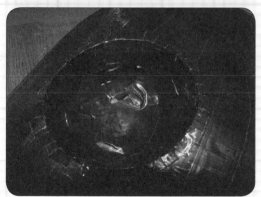

Step 23: Fold Tape

Fold the tape to form 3 small loops and place them evenly spaced around the brim.

Step 24: Finish

Fold each of the 3 tape loops into the crown. Enjoy your duct tape pirate hat. Arrrrr!

Cardboard and Duct Tape Viking Helmet

By Duct Crossing

www.instructables.com/id/Cardboard-
and-Duct-Tape-Viking-Helmet/

This guide will teach you how to make a Viking helmet out of nothing but duct tape and cardboard (and some other stuff).

Step 1: Materials

For this project, you will need the following:

- Single-ply corrugated cardboard
- Brown, "cookie," and gray duct tape (or whatever colors you want—it's your helmet)
- Balloon
- Measuring tape
- Newspaper
- Normal tape
- Scissors
- Hot glue

Step 2: Measuring

First, measure your head. Now make a thin strip of non-sticky duct tape the same length. I encountered some smallness issues, so you might want to add on an inch or so.

Now take the strip and tape the ends together. If it's right, the strip should fit around your head like a headband.

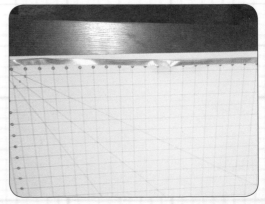

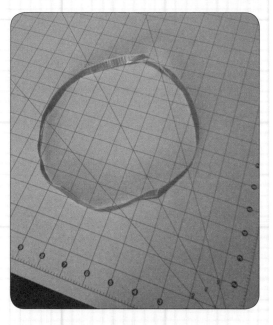

Step 3: Choosing Your Victim

Now, choose the unfortunate balloon to build on. Blow it up inside the "headband" so that it'll be nice and tight. However, don't blow it up so tight that the balloon pops.

Step 4: Taping

Now, put tape sticky side up all over the helmet area. At first, I tried to stick the pieces underneath the headband, but that took too long, so I wrapped a piece sticky side up around the headband. Try to not let many air bubbles form.

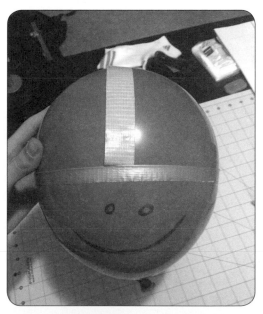

Step 5: Cutting Cardboard

If you are reading this step, then you have completed the long boring work and you're ready for some more long boring work. Cut out a bunch of cardboard triangles. How many you need depends on the size of your head. Let's just say I was cutting for a while. Put the triangles all around the sticky hat like so.

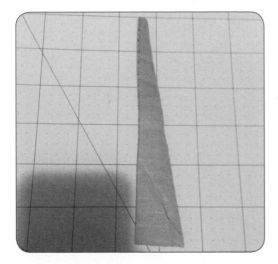

Step 6: More Taping

Congratulations! You have struggled through all that cardboard cutting! Are you ready for some more mindless taping?

Cover the whole helmet with the color you have chosen for the helmet. Once you have completed that, it's time to pop the balloon. If you came to this page to make half of a coconut or cover up a bad haircut, stop here. Those who want to make a Viking helmet, continue on to step 7.

Step 7: Making Horns

Do any trimming you need to do and put tape on the ends. Once you're done with that, get out the newspaper! I made the horns by bending tubes of newspaper and adding wads to fill in the creases.

Your horns don't have to look like mine—after all, it's your helmet. Once they're built, cover them in the tape of your choosing.

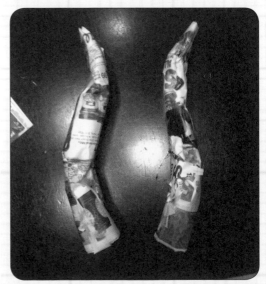

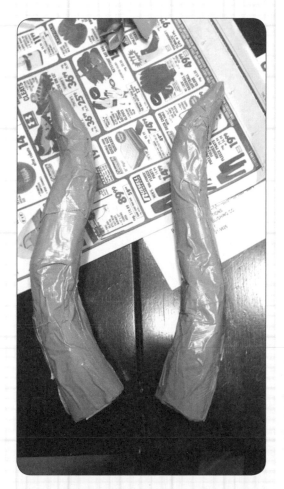

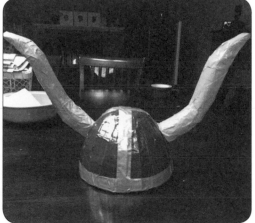

Step 8: Attaching Horns

Glue *and* tape the horns onto your helmet. Then add some detail.

Step 9: Enjoy!

Now you have your very own Viking helmet! Now get out there and raid and pillage! (On second thought, don't. They'll arrest you.)

I find it very difficult to find a hat that will fit my head just right, especially since I wear a pony tail most of the time. So this design allowed me to create a hat the perfect size for me!

Step 1: Fitting the Hat

Measure with a piece of string the circumference of your head; this is where the bottom of the hat will lay, so consider where you want your hat to rest, Also, don't forget about your ears. I always have hats that are too small to include my pony tail, so I was sure to include that in my calculation.

Now cut a piece of duct tape of that length and fold it in half the long way so that the sticky sides come together. Make a circle with that piece of tape and then tape it together.

Now measure, with a piece of string, from the front of your forehead to the back of your head. Imagine this is going to form the top of your hat, so you will not want to make it too small or too large. Again, cut a piece of duct tape to this length and then fold it in half the long way so that the sticky side will be on the inside. Now cut another piece this same length and do the same thing to it as you did to the pieces before. Make an X with those 2 pieces and tape them together. Then take the ends of the 2 pieces used to make

an X and tape the ends to the circle that you made in the beginning.

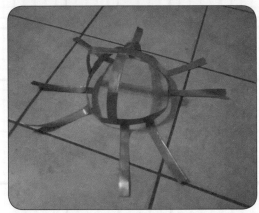

Step 2: Brim of the Hat

Now we will be making the frame for the brim of the sun hat. Think about how long you want your brim to be. Mine is about 6 inches long, but you can try making it as long or as short as you want to. Measure out a piece of duct tape that is the length of the brim that you want (in my case, 6 inches), and fold it in half the long way so that the sticky side is facing in, just like we did for all for all of the other pieces that we made so far. Now make about 8 of these, or as many as you'd like. They will outline the brim of your hat.

Once you have these brim pieces cut and taped together, tape them to the bottom of your hat frame so that they stick out (like the brim of a sun hat). Once they are all attached, cut pieces of tape that are folded in half and tape a circle around the outside of those little brim pieces. See photos for help.

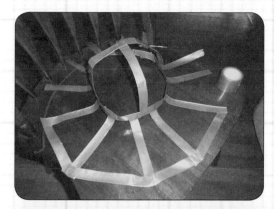

Step 3: Finishing It Up!

Now cut rather large pieces of tape and stick them on your hat so that they fill in all of the gaps. Make sure that the tape that you use on the outside of the hat will be the color that you want the hat to be. I chose a navy blue tape for my hat's outside and a silver tape for the hat's inside.

Keep in mind that this hat is made out of tape, so make sure that there are no sticky parts exposed, especially on the inside.

Sports, Games, and Outdoor Activities

This ball can be used as a super-light volleyball, playground ball, or just a ball to play catch with. You might find other uses as well. The ball is light and grippy. It's cheap and easy to make. It is surprisingly durable and stands up to repeated kicking.

Step 1: Materials

Gather your materials.
You will need:

- Two 12-inch balloons
- A roll of duct tape
- If desired, a different color roll of duct tape for decoration (not shown)

We used 2 balloons, one inside the other, for extra support and strength.

Step 2: Balloons

Turn one of the balloons inside-out. I discovered that the inside of the balloon is dustier and less grippy.

Step 3: Twist Balloon

Twist the balloon you turned inside-out like shown. Make sure the balloon has no air inside.

Step 4: Double Up Balloons

Insert the twisted balloon into the other balloon.

Step 5: Folding

Fold the top of the inner balloon onto the outer balloon, like shown.

Step 6: Blow Up Balloon

Blow up the inner balloon and tie a knot on the top.

Step 7: Duct Tape

Start covering the balloon in duct tape. Be sure to pull it especially tight over the knot. If you put all the duct tape on tightly enough, the ball will be round.

Step 8: Done!

Congratulations! You have completed your duct tape ball!

Step 9: Optional

Decorate the ball with another color of duct tape.

The following steps provide a simple and effective means of using supplies attainable for little to no money to create a full, usable chess set. While these steps illustrate the means by which I conducted this project, they are in no way exclusive, and I urge you to customize the project based on your personal desires.

Step 1: Gathering the Materials

The first step in the process of creating this project is to gather the materials necessary to build the components of a chess set.

Materials for constructing the board:
- 3 rolls of duct tape (2 rolls for the board, 1 for looks and structure)
- USPS medium size standard rate box (or another box with at least one square side)
- Scissors
- Sharpie marker
- Ruler or meter stick

Materials for constructing the chess pieces:
- Remainder of the 3 rolls of duct tape
- 2 packs of different colored pipe cleaners
- 36 spare coins (mixture of quarters, nickels, and pennies—no dimes)
- Scissors

Step 2: Marking the Square Surface

The first step in creating the board that the game will be played on is to create a grid-like pattern on the square bottom surface of the USPS box. To do this, take the measuring implement, either a ruler or meter stick, and separate the length and width of the box into 8 even-sized areas on each side This means drawing 7 lines across the width of the box at even intervals (see picture for clarification). Using the Sharpie, darken the lines to the point where they can be easily seen through a thin piece of white printer paper.

When you have finished this, you should have a grid-like pattern across the bottom of the box. The pictures below show a decent example.

Step 3: Beginning the Alternating Chess Coloring

The next step is the process of repeatedly overlapping squares of different colored duct tape on top of one another to create a repeating pattern of alternating colors that correspond to the grid created in the previous step. To begin this pattern, cut a piece of white duct tape that is just slightly larger than a single square. Place it in one corner of the square grid, aiming to place it as close to in line with the edge as possible.

Next, cut an equal-sized square of a different colored duct tape (red in the pictures) and lay it along the grid line that you can see through the white tape. Both squares will slightly overlap the grid lines. This is fine, as the additional tape will ensure that none of the lines show through the pieces of tape.

Continue this pattern along the rest of the grid until you have finished the row. (See picture for clarification.) Fold over the additional tape at the end of the row and then turn your attention back to where you began.

The second row will begin with a square that is the opposite color of the one with which you began the row above. When repeated, this will create the alternating grid pattern that is evident in commercial chess boards. Finish the row, and repeat this process throughout the remainder of the rows.

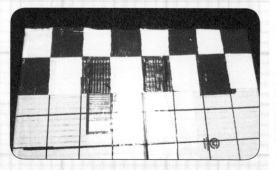

Step 4: Finishing the Grid

Continue overlapping the squares repeatedly until the entire surface is covered and appears as a red and white alternating grid. Because I used thinner duct tape, I decided that it was pertinent to add an additional layer of duct tape to the grid already down, mostly for appearance's sake. This also ensured a more level playing ground, as the dual tape layers re-enforced the cardboard below it.

Step 5: Taping the Sides

For appearance's sake, as well as to protect the cardboard from spills and wear and tear, I felt it was necessary to wrap the sides that were not a part of the grid with a layer of duct tape. To do this, simply wrap layer after layer of duct tape (black in my case) around the edges and sides of the box. Repeat this process for the whole of the uncovered box, making sure to overlap the edges of the long strips so that no cardboard shows. Also continue this process for the bottom of the box, using long strips laid in a single direction to ensure efficiency and a good appearance. (See photos for clarification.)

Step 6: Gather Materials for the Pieces

For the pieces, you will need to gather the previously mentioned materials. For the duct tape requirement, use what remains of the previous duct tape rolls, as it should be more than is necessary. Gather also the different colored pipe cleaner packs, as well as at least 36 spare coins, ensuring that they are a mixture of pennies, quarters, and nickels. You will also need a pair of scissors for the customization of each piece.

Step 7: Creating a Basic Piece

Now that you have created an acceptable board, it is time to create a matching chess set out of coins, duct tape, and pipe cleaners. To begin, lay a piece of tape (which should be a rough square) out with the adhesive side facing up, away from the surface of the table. Next, lay one coin at the center of the square. Take a small length of pipe cleaner (roughly 4 inches in length) and bend it slightly at one end before placing it in the center of the coin on the table. Using the edges of the tape lying on the table, fold them inward and across the bent pipe cleaner section, effectively holding it in place. For the pawns, this was the extent of work, though I did bend the protruding length of pipe cleaner, which was roughly 3 inches long, into a spiral to give it dimension. For the more specialized pieces, I altered the means by which I added their unique characteristics. This will be discussed in following steps. (See pictures for clarification.)

For the opposing series of chess pieces, I used white tape (as opposed to red) and white pipe cleaners (as opposed to black), but the steps were the same.

Step 8: Customizing the Individual Pieces

In order to customize the pieces based on their specific purpose, I added a simple piece of tape to the top of the pipe cleaner and shaped it using scissors so that each piece was easily identifiable. While I will not describe the process for each individual piece (as at this point I encourage as much customization as possible), I have included a picture of the different customizations I made. The single enlarged piece is the red queen, which I added so you could have an enlarged view of a single piece.

I apologize for the difficulty in seeing the white pieces. The general shape of each piece is as follows:

- Castle: Twisted pipe cleaner upward in a cylinder-like shape
- Knight: Slight bend meant to resemble the head of a horse after slight twist for dimension
- Bishop: Pope-like cap above curled pipe-cleaner, like a bent staff
- Queen: Red: jagged to personify chaos; White: large circle to personify order
- King: Red: 3-pronged for chaos; White: cross for order

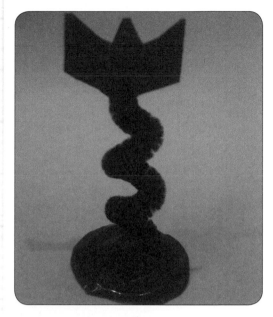

Step 9: Finished Set

Following the customization of the pieces, continue with completing the set. A full set will include 16 pawns (8 white, 8 red), 4 castles (2 white, 2 red), 4 knights (2 white, 2 red), 4 bishops (2 white, 2 red), 2 queens (1 white, 1 red), and 2 kings (1 white, 1 red), for a total of 32 pieces. Once you have filled in the blanks, simply place the pieces on the board and you are ready to play. The weighted bottoms will cause the pieces to tend towards the righted position, meaning that the chess set can be played even in places where you may be bumped or jostled.

Congratulations, you have now completed your own personalized, duct tape chess set! I urge you to go into the customization aspect of this project far more in depth then I have.

As an additional note, a small cut can be made in the bottom of the box, allowing the pieces to be stored inside the hollow USPS box quite effectively. In addition, spare duct tape and pipe cleaners can be stored inside for quick fixes and even more customization.

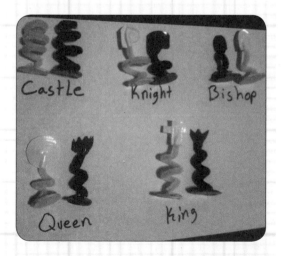

This kite is awesome and it is easy to make! The materials used in this Instructable are commonly found at home; if not, you will probably find them at the closest supermarket.

Step 1: Tools and Materials

- Newspaper
- Some kind of thread (my choice was dental floss)
- Scissors
- 3 skewers
- Some kind of tool to cut the skewers
- Duct tape

Step 2: The Fabric

You might be asking yourself, "Why didn't he just use 2 sheets of duct tape fabric instead of newspaper?" Well, the reason why I used newspaper instead of duct tape was because it would be way too heavy—newspaper is light so it is just perfect. Start by covering the newspaper in strips of duct tape, covering almost the whole sheet.

Step 3: Mark the Kite

Now mark the outside of the kite. From top to bottom: 24 cm; from left to right: 22.8 cm; lastly, from top to where the 2 lines cross: 5 cm. Then just outline the figure.

Step 4: Cut Skewers

Using your drawing as a guideline, cut your skewers. Put one on top of the other and then line them up to the drawing. Then we have to attach the 2 skewers to each other, for which we will use duct tape. Now this does not have to look pretty; all that really matters is that they stick well together.

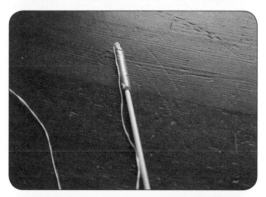

Step 5: The Line of the Kite

What we will start with here is making some grooves in the skewers so that the thread sits still. But before we begin that, I have to say be careful! Even though you have many years experience of making small grooves, you can cut yourself! Small children should be under parental supervision if they use a sharp object.

Anyways, back to the build! Make grooves on each corner. You can do this with almost any sharp tool. Put the string on the bottom groove, the tape it in a way that it will stay there for a long time. Use a lot of tape for this part. It is important that the bottom is heavy, because it has to be stable. Keep working your way over the 3 other corners, taping it down as you move toward the end. When you come down to where you started, tape it down excessively.

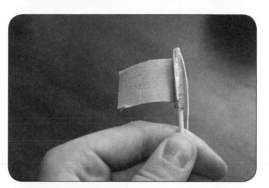

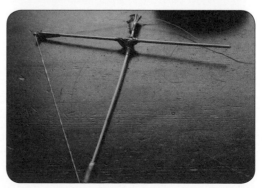

Step 6: Put It on the Other Side

The 4 different points need to be transferred to the other side, because we want the duct tape side facing out. The way I did this was using a pen and poking through the 4 points so that they show up on the other side. Then I used a ruler and drew lines connecting the dots.

Step 7: Cutting

Now cut the whole thing out, 2½ cm from the line. Don't throw the remaining fabric away just yet, as we will need it later. Line the wooden pieces up to the drawing and use tape to secure it over the line and to the body, as shown in the pictures.

Step 8: The Tail

Cut a piece of string (about 57 cm). Now cut some squares out of the fabric (7 cm by 3 cm). Then squish them so that they kind of look like a small bow tie. Make 4 of these with about 7 cm in between each.

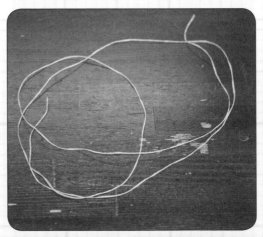

Step 9: Finishing

Cut a 12½ cm long string, and then attach it to the vertical skewer. Next, attach the rest of the string on the spool to that the vertical skewer, then put a skewer through the spool.

I decided to make an old-school baseball glove, inspired by Roy Hobbs of *The Natural*. The goal was to make the glove 100 percent from duct tape.

Step 1: Template

A template was made from poster board by tracing my hand, then tracing a larger area to create the glove. Tape was overlaid and placed face to face to create 2 sheets. The template was then traced onto these sheets and cut using scissors.

Step 2: Stitching

The 2 glove pieces were placed together and all the seams bound using duct tape.

Step 3: Inside Out

Once the binding was done, the glove was turned inside out to hide all the tape seams. This was the most difficult part of the process, taking a lot of time and effort. To pull the fingers all the way through I had to use needle-nose pliers to grab the tips, being careful not to rip the tape.

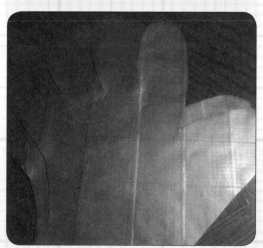

Step 4: Webbing

The strips for the webbing were created by folding strips of duct tape over 3 times. Notches were cut in the back of the thumb and index finger, and the strips were threaded through. The ends of the strips were peeled back, and the excess flap was removed and then folded over to adhere to the notch and strip.

Step 5: Lacing

Holes for the laces were made using a wooden skewer. The lacing was done the same way as the webbing—folded over duct tape with thin strips cut with scissors. The lacing was pushed through the holes using the wooden skewer.

Step 6: Finished

I added a lightning bolt for that "Wonderboy" touch. I don't know if I'd use this for catching baseballs, but it should help improve one's fielding percentage on the wiffle ball field.

Duct Tape Game Board (Chess, Draughts, and Backgammon)

By Slamdunk

www.instructables.com/id/
Duct-Tape-Game-Board-Chess%2c-
Draughts-and-Backgamm/

This Instructable shows you how to make a game board for chess, draughts (checkers in American English), and backgammon from duct tape.

Step 1: Bin Bag Foundation

As a foundation for the board, cut a black bin liner up so that you have a square of plastic at least 12 times the width of your duct tape (60cm in my case). Duct tape the plastic to your work bench so that it is lightly tensioned. Then stretch alternate color strips of duct tape across the plastic as shown in the photo. Make sure that the edges of the tape are as close as possible without overlapping.

Step 2: Slice 'n' Dice

Next, mark the edge of the outer 2 bits of tape at regular intervals the same distance apart as the tape is wide (about 5cm in my case). Then, using a ruler and a sharp craft knife, slice the strips across the so that you have separate strips of alternating color tape. You should end up with 8 strips.

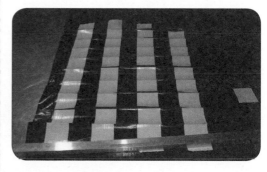

Step 3: Shuffle the Deck

Rotate every other strip through 180 degrees and replace it where it came from so that you have alternating color squares.

Step 4: As If by Magic

Duct tape the strips to the workbench again so that they line up with the edges as close as possible without overlapping. Magic tape the internal edges and across the strips for strength. Add some strips of a third color of tape to either end so that the board is rectangular—about 10 percent longer than it is wide. Forty-five by 55cm is tournament backgammon size, so if you're picky then this is your target size.

Step 5: Flip It

Carefully remove the board from the workbench, leaving all of the tape in place, and turn it over. Tape it back to the workbench with the underside face up.

Step 6: The Invisible Step

If you're a real duct tape ninja then you might be able to skip this step. Since this was my first duct tape build I used clear, sticky-back plastic to keep the parts constructed so far in place. It's difficult to see in the photo, but it's there if you look closely.

Step 7: To the Bar

The first step in making the backgammon side of the board is to add the center bar in the middle—2cm wide in my case, but make it in proportion to the tape (two-fifths the width of your tape).

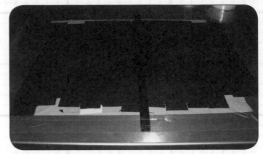

Step 8: Complete Cover-Up

Complete the base of the backgammon side of the board with strips of duct tape in your third color. Again, make sure that the edges of the tape touch but do not overlap.

Step 9: Look, No Safety Net

Carefully remove the board from the workbench again and remove your Magic tape safety net from the chessboard side.

Step 10: Cut to Size and Edge

Next, trim the board down so that the long sides only have half the width of your tape in extra material on either side of the chess board. Then wrap tape around this extra material to finish the long edges. Don't finish the short edges yet! This allows for some variance in the width of your backgammon triangles.

Step 11: The Triangular Step

Make 24 triangles of duct tape, 12 one color and 12 another. They should be 10 percent narrower than the tape and a bit shorter than the width of the board.

Step 12: Fix the Triangles

Fix the triangles along the long edges of the backgammon side of the board so that they alternate in color across the length and width of the board.

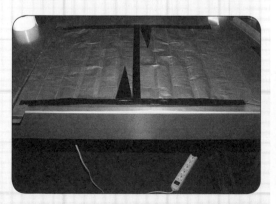

Step 13: Almost There . . .

This is what the backgammon side of the board should look like with all the triangles attached. It doesn't seem to matter if you start with the lighter color on the right of the bar or on the left.

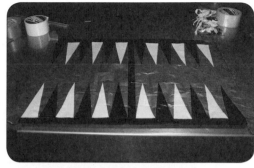

Step 14: Finished!

Finish the board by folding tape over the short edges of the board. You can add corner reinforcement too if you like.

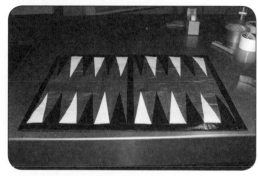

Step 15: Checkmate!

Here in all its wrinkly glory is the finished board chess-side up. Happy gaming!

Woven Duct Tape Berry-Picking Basket

By susanrm

www.instructables.com/id/Woven-Duct-Tape-Berry-Picking-Basket/

I live in an area where lots of berries grow wild, and I love to pick them. So I decided to make a berry-picking basket to make the process easier. Duct tape makes it colorful and easy.

Step 1: You Will Need

- 2 rolls of duct tape in contrasting colors
- Acetate or transparencies
- Cutter
- Measuring mat and/or tape measure

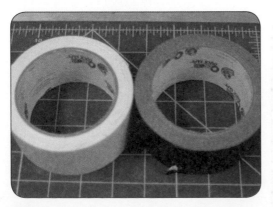

Step 2: Preparation

To start the body of the basket, tear off ten 11-inch strips of duct tape in one color and fold them in half to form strips approximately 1 inch in width. Make twenty 5- to 6-inch folded strips the same way in a contrasting color.

Step 3: Weaving

Place 5 long strips on your table and tape down with a strip of duct tape (I use the plain gray kind to save the good, expensive stuff). Weave 10 short strips. To keep the weave tight, use bits of duct tape to hold the strips in place as you weave them.

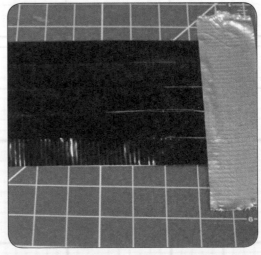

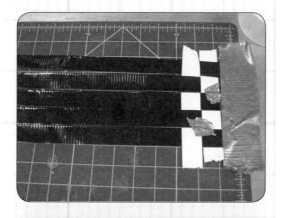

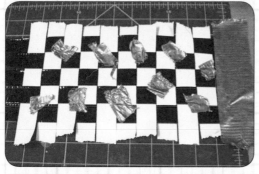

Step 4: Lining

Remove the strip holding the weaving to the table and flip the weaving over. Place strips of duct tape along the back of the weaving to line it in one solid color. (I recommend a darker color, as berries might stain a light one.) When this step is finished, turn the sheet back over and remove the bits of ugly duct tape. Then cut around the edges to square off your sheet to one solid woven rectangle.

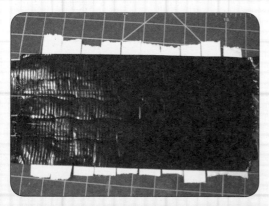

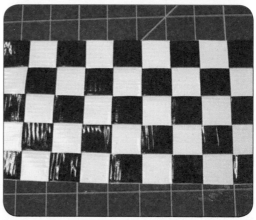

Step 5: Repeat

Repeat the previous steps with your remaining strips. You will now have 2 woven sheets with solid lining on the back.

Step 6: Attach Walls

Attach the 2 walls of the basket by lining up the sides and putting a piece of duct tape on the outside and one inside. Do this twice. You should end up with a circle at the end.

The reason I don't weave this all as one big piece is that the longer the duct tape pieces get, the easier they are to wrinkle or ruin.

Step 7: Make the Bottom

Fold the walls every 5 squares so you have a square box. Measure the area of the box; it should be about 5 inches by 5 inches. Make a duct tape sheet slightly larger than that by tearing off pieces that are around 6 inches long, placing 3 with the sticky sides up then 3 more on top of them.

Cut the square bottom so it will fit your basket. Tape the bottom to the basket. Ideally, overlap the colored tape so it goes exactly over the bottom row of squares. Do the outside first, then the inside.

The inside step can be a bit tricky; take your time, and remember, it doesn't have to be perfect. First, tear pieces a bit under 5 inches long and place them one at a time inside over the seam. I find it helps, before placing them, to fold them with the sticky side out and placing the fold on the seam.

Step 8: Tape the Top Edges

Using pieces around 5 inches long again, tape around the top edges of the basket.

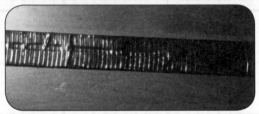

Step 9: Make the Strap

Use a tape measure or a string to measure the length over your shoulder so the basket will sit on your hip. Add about 8 inches for attaching the strap. I ended up with a 44-inch strap.

To make a sturdy strap, I like to cut 1-inch strips of transparencies (the kind used in overhead projectors) for shaping and strength. I cut 5 strips (11 inches long each).

Carefully tear off a length of duct tape that equals the length of the strap you want. Without allowing it to fold or stick to itself, lay it sticky side up. Place the transparency strips down the middle of it, overlapping so there are no gaps. Fold over the edges. They will not completely cover the transparency.

Then tear off another strip of the same length. Lay it sticky-side up and place the strap ugly-side down on it. Fold the sticky edges over the strap again. You will now have a nice strap.

Step 10: Attach the Strap

Attach the strap to the inside of the basket with duct tape. Bring it as far down to the bottom as you can, making sure it is still comfortable to sling over your shoulder. If it is too long, you can either cut it or run it along the bottom of the basket as well. Secure with duct tape, but don't go crazy on this unless you plan on carrying heavier things than berries.

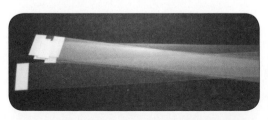

Step 11: Finished—Go Berry Picking!

This basket makes it super easy to just pick and place the berries. If you want to keep the inside clean, put a produce bag inside it (I wash and reuse mine). Then you will have a ready-made bag of berries. You can also bring multiple bags, like at the height of raspberry season, and use the basket for picking and the bags for storing and carrying home. Enjoy!

School and Office Supplies

Duct Tape Binder

By moskiii13
www.instructables.com/id/
Duct-tape-Binder/

Have an old binder that is falling apart? Or do you just want to add some style to your school supplies? This tutorial will help you reuse your old binders and make them one of a kind!

Step 1: What You Need
• A binder
• Some duct tape
• Scissors (optional)

Step 2: First . . .
Measure a strip of duct tape to fit the inside of your binder. It's good to start in the inside because then there will be no loose pieces on the outside when you finish. If you have a pocket on the inside, measure the pocket first.

Step 3: More
Add more strips to the pocket.

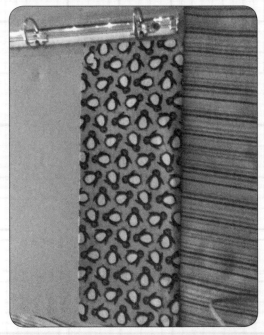

Step 4: The Real Thing
Now we get on to the bigger part of the binder. Take a strip of duct tape and measure it to the rest of the inside (making sure it overlaps the top and the pocket a little).

Step 5: Tuck

Tuck the remainder of the tape underneath the pocket and wrap the top around to the front.

Step 6: Continue

Do the same thing all the way down the binder.

Step 7: Mirrored

Do the same thing to the other half of the binder.

Step 8: Front

The front is probably a little covered already, but we will cover it all the way. Take your duct tape and cover the front. If there is extra, make sure you only fold on the top, not the bottom, because then there would be random colors on the pocket.

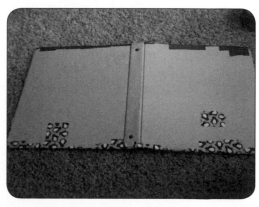

Step 9: Copy

Do the same thing to the other side.

Step 11: Personalize!

Add your own design to it! It doesn't matter what it is, just be creative.

Step 10: The Middle

You can use regular pieces for the middle, but it makes the binder close oddly. Take a strip as long as the binder and cut it in half. The photos should explain the rest.

Duct Tape Pencil Grip

By Jessie Marie
www.instructables.com/id/
Duct-Tape-Pencil-Grip/

Here is a simple, easy way to make a pencil grip in less than 5 minutes with the one material everyone has: good ol' duct tape! You can make an assortment of these pencil grips in no time, varying in color and size. The best part about these is that if you like your pencil grips thick, you can make them that way. If not, it's okay; you just won't use as many layers of duct tape, making a thinner pencil grip. The thing about duct tape is that it is really strong and just as good as any other material. It is cheaper, too! With these instructions, you can make a sturdy pencil grip customized for your very own pencil!

Step 1: Materials
- Duct tape (patterned tape works best)
- Pencil

Step 2: Wrap the Pencil Sticky Side Out

For starters, determine the length you want your pencil grip to be. It is easier to just go with the standard width of the duct tape, but if you like the challenge, go right ahead! Take a strip of duct tape sticky side out and wrap it tightly, but not too tightly that it can't slide up and down,

and not too loose that it slides right off the pencil. Remember, the sticky side should be out.

Step 3: Wrap More Tape On

Next, wrap duct tape (sticky side in, like normal) around the sticky base of the pencil grip. You may want to do this in sections in case the duct tape gets positioned wrong. The more tape you wrap around the pencil grip, the thicker it will be.

Step 4: You're Done!

Now, unless you are going to go ahead and start using the grip right away, slide off the pencil grip from your pencil, and admire how sturdy it is and how many of these you could make in such a little amount of time! Give them to your friends or keep them for yourself. Experiment with different colors, patterns, and thicknesses to vary what your outcome may be!

Heart-Shaped Box

By Random_Canadian
www.instructables.com/id/
Heart-Shaped-Box-1/

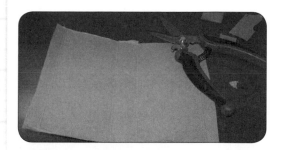

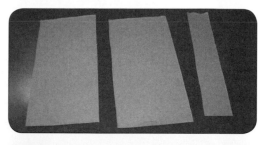

No glue . . . just recycled cardboard and duct tape!

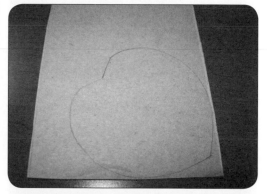

Step 1: Tools and Materials
- Duct tape
- Cardboard
- Scissors
- Hobby knife
- Drawing implement

Step 2: Free Form

The heart is free form and cut from a piece of an old food box that was destined for the bin. You will need 2 heart shapes, one slightly larger than the other.

Since these will have to nest together, make sure that the larger one is big enough to make room for the cardboard core and tape layers.

Cut the smaller heart from cardboard, then flip it over and trace the edge on another piece. Cut the larger one about 2mm outside of the edge of the smaller one.

Trim any folds with a hobby knife. Flatten and cover all exposed cardboard with duct tape. Keep all tape as smooth as possible.

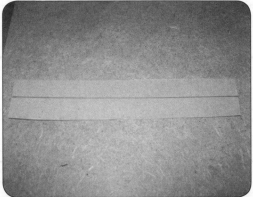

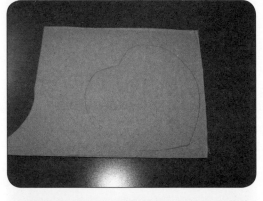

Step 3: Box Top

Cut 2 strips of cardboard that are 1 cm wide. Use several small strips of tape to secure the strips around the edge of the larger heart. Add more tape to secure the strips. Cover all the exposed cardboard with tape strips.

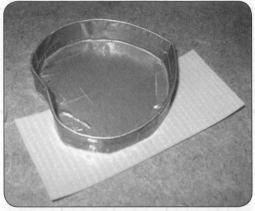

Step 4: The Box

Repeat the same procedure with the box bottom, only this time use strips that are wide enough to accommodate the height of what you wish to place inside of the box.

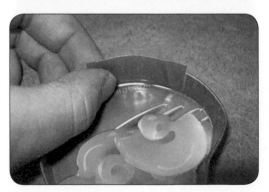

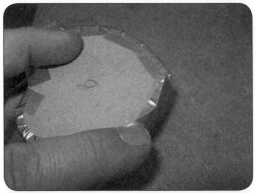

Step 5: Make It Pretty

Add a final layer of duct tape in the color of your choice. Make it as smooth as possible.

Step 6: Add Contrast

If you are adding a decoration to the top of the box, you should add a contrast color so that the decoration is not lost in the background.

134

Step 7: Make a Rose

You will need to use several square sections of the tape color of your choice. Fold one corner in as shown. Fold an adjacent corner in as shown, trim the point round, and roll the center petal into a tight cylinder. Add a second petal to the roll but fold small sections of the sticky section near the "stem" together to create texture.

Continue wrapping petals and folding the base to cause the petals to flare out from the center. Add as many petals as desired until the rose takes shape.

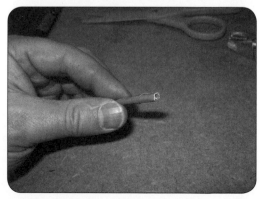

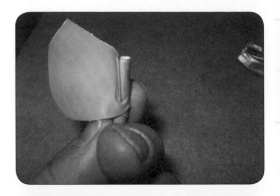

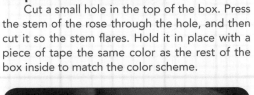

Step 8: Mount the Rose

Cut a small hole in the top of the box. Press the stem of the rose through the hole, and then cut it so the stem flares. Hold it in place with a piece of tape the same color as the rest of the box inside to match the color scheme.

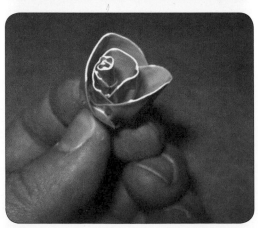

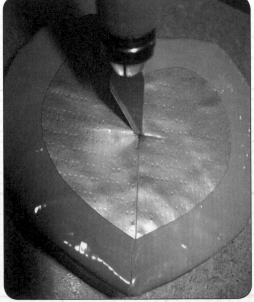

How to Make a Duct Tape Laptop Sleeve/ Cover

By innvert
www.instructables.com/id/
How-to-make-a-Duck-tape-Laptop-
computer-sleeve-c/

I was in need of a laptop sleeve for my computer but wanted to construct my own. This is how to make one easily on a cheap budget.

Step 1: Materials

- 2 rolls of duct tape (different colors recommended)
- Sharp knife or scissors
- Place for cutting (e.g., cutting board)
- Laptop for measurement

Step 2: Duct Tape Sheet

Measure the width and length of your computer. Start constructing a duct tape sheet. A duct tape sheet is made by laying strips of duct tape next to each other adhesive side up with no space between them, then placing another strip in the middle of those pieces adhesive side down. Repeat this process until you have a sheet of it, making sure the length is larger than the computer.

Note: When constructing this, try alternating the colors of the tape in order to give a nice pattern. I used blue and black.

Step 3: Duct Tape Sheet

Make the sheet so it is double the length of the laptop from front to back. Find the center strip and reinforce the base for strength. Once you have made the sheet so it can completely cover the laptop, do a couple more strips as a cover/lid for the sleeve so it overlaps the other side.

Step 4: Sides

To clean up the sides of the duct tape sheet, place a strip of tape on the edges with some adhesive exposed and then fold over to give it a nice look.

138

Step 5: Finish Sides

Place your laptop on the sleeve and fold the side so the computer fits snugly, then remove the computer and tape the sides closed. Next, tape the inside edges of the sleeves for strength. I found the top flap became larger than the case, as I had folded the sides in, so I trimmed it a little to fit.

Step 6: Lid/Cover

Edge the top the same way as the sides to give it a nice, clean look.

Step 7: Optional Handle

The handle is optional. I did not make one, but it is easily done. Choose the size you want your handle to be and attach a strip of tape to the inside edges of the bag with the adhesive side out. Then attach a piece to the outside, attaching it to the other strap. You can reinforce it as much as you want for strength. Do not attach to the lid, as the lid is flimsy and is not supportive enough.

Step 8: Results

Here are some final pictures from my bag.

Duct Tape Bookmark

By beme2013

www.instructables.com/id/
Duct-Tape-Bookmark-2/

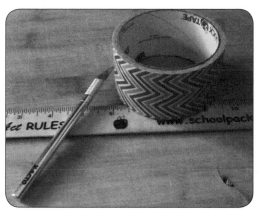

Step 1: What You'll Need

For this project you will need:

- Duct tape
- X-Acto knife or scissors
- A ruler
- A hard surface (The reason why you need a hard surface is so you can stick and unstick tape on it and because it's pretty handy if you're using an X-Acto knife. I use a cutting board, but you can use a cutting board or cutting mat. Just don't use the kitchen table or counter. You don't want cut marks all over your furniture.)

Step 2: Cut

Cut 2 strips of tape that are each 6 inches long.

Step 3: Stick Them Together

Flip one strip over so that the sticky side faces upwards. Then take the other strip and put it on the first piece, sticky side to sticky side. And you're done!

Duct Tape Book Cover

By hailtothkngbby
www.instructables.com/id/
Duct-tape-Book-Cover/

This describes in detail how to create a book cover out of the most useful tool known to mankind: duct tape.

Step 1: Materials

- A book
- Duct tape
- Scissors
- Marker
- Tape measure (not necessary, but helpful)

Step 2: Preparation

First, measure your book (height x width). My book is 9½ inches tall by 17 inches wide. To find the proper width, you need to open your book about halfway. This should lay both the front and the back cover on the table, along with the spine. The covers on my book are both 7½ inches, and the spine is 2 inches. Voila, 17 inches.

Next, we need to decide the size of our sheet. I added 4 inches total to the height and 10 inches to the total width. That makes our total about 14 by 27 inches.

Finally, clean off your work surface. Gather your supplies.

Step 3: Make the Sheet

Making the sheet is pretty simple. Since our total height is 14 inches and our roll of duct tape is 2 inches wide, we'd need 7 strips to make the height—7 strips at 27 inches long. To make this easier I took my tape measure and measured a spot 27 inches from the edge of the table and put a small piece of tape there as a measurement guide. Make sure you are not doing this on a good piece of furniture, as duct tape *will* pull the finish off of some wood.

Next, I pulled 7 strips off the roll, each about 27 inches long. Remember, you get no points for perfection here. I laid each of these strips (sticky side up) out edge to edge, making a 14-inch by 27-inch series of strips. I call these the "field strips." To hold them together you will need 8 more strips that are 27 inches long. I call these "binding strips."

Start by placing the first binding strip half on the first field strip and half on the second field strip. Make sure these are *sticky side down*. Continue this with 5 more binding strips and you should have 1 inch of sticky side showing on the top and bottom. Then take the last 2 binders and place one sticky side down, half on the first field strip, half on the table, the last one goes half on the last field strip, half on the table, sticky side down. Take a straight edge and make a line along both side edges and cut along the line to make a nice, straight rectangle. Then you're going to flip the sheet over. You should have 1 inch of sticky side showing at the top and bottom. Fold both sticky sides inward to make a nice folded-over edge on both the top and the bottom.

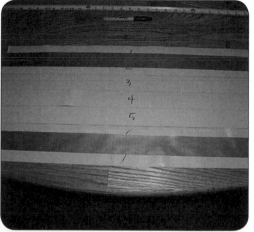

There you have it: a 14-inch by 27-inch sheet of duct tape.

Step 4: In the Fold

Okay, we're almost done now. Lay out your sheet. Mark 2 inches up from the bottom and 2 inches down from the top. I used the book to make a nice straight line. Be careful not to mark the book, as they are very expensive. Then remove the book and fold the sheet on the lines you just made. Set the book back down to hold the folds in place.

Step 5: Side Pockets

Next you're going to open the book about halfway again, laying it evenly on the sheet. Try to leave about the same amount on both sides, about 5 inches each. Go ahead and mark the sheet again where the book covers end.

Now close the book and open only the front cover. Fold the left side of the sheet along the line and insert it into the pocket that is formed by the flaps. Push it in all the way to the fold, and then close the book so that the back cover is facing up. Take this opportunity to stabilize the flaps by placing a piece of duct tape on each flap, taping the flap down to the sheet where the spine will sit. This helps to keep the flaps from unfolding during prolonged or rough use.

Now open the back cover only. Fold the right side of the sheet inward on the fold line. Duct tape is flexible enough that you can insert the back cover into its pocket with little trouble. Push the cover all the way into the pocket to the fold. Then close the book.

Next, take a couple pieces of tape and fold them over the edge of the cover to hold the pocket firmly against the cover (front and back, top and bottom).

Step 6: Labels!

Since very few people can see through duct tape, we will attach some labels! You could write all over this cover—the one you just spent an hour on. Or, you could write on a separate piece of tape and place it on the cover and the spine, thereby making this cover reusable. It takes very little effort to reuse this on smaller books, and only the addition of a couple strips to reuse it on a larger book! It's worth it. These covers age like a good concert t-shirt.

top third down. This makes something like a tape-on tail.

Next, take your "tail" and tape it, using the 2-inch by 2-inch sticky part, to the lowest part of the spine of the book, leaving the slender portion to dangle. Lastly, take a piece about 6 inches long and tape over the sticky square for added support. Start by putting 2 inches of it on the front cover, next to your tail attachment point, and then wrap it around, pressing firmly all the way to the back cover.

Step 7: Book Tail

No, we're not making a book tail—it's a book mark! This is everyone's favorite part of this cover. Here's what you do: Take a strip of duct tape, about 5 inches longer than your book is tall. Mine is about 14 inches. Next, 2 inches in from one end make 2 marks. If the strip is lying in front of you left to right, you will make your 2 marks vertically, one coming down from the top one-third the width of the tape and one coming up from the bottom one-third the width. See photo. This is very important. Each mark is only one-third of the tape's width. Now, cut along those marks. This releases the edges of the strip, leaving the 2-inch by 2-inch piece, which is attached to the larger piece by only one-third of the strip. Fold the bottom third of the long piece up, then follow by folding the

Step 8: Enjoy!

Now take your book to school, and enjoy it when everyone asks you to make them one.

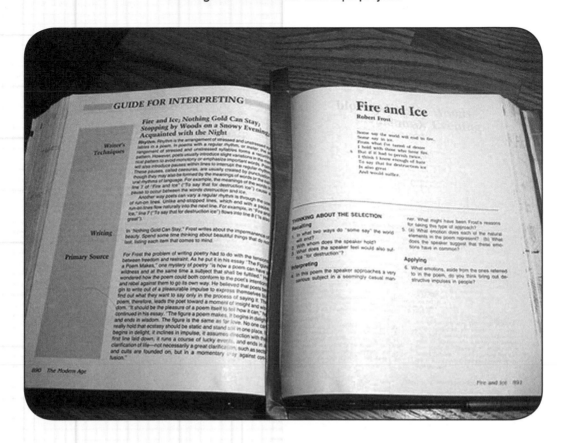

Creatures

Duct Tape Figures

By bikeparts24

www.instructables.com/id/
Duct-Tape-Figures/

These bendable figures are great for making stop-action movies because they are easy to make, they hold their shape, and with magnets, they can stick to metal.

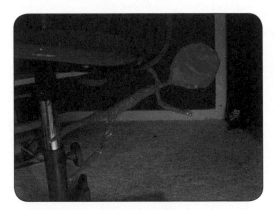

Step 1: What You Need

- Bendable wire
- Duct tape (different colors if you want)
- Wire cutters
- Scissors
- Something round that is as big as you want the head to be. (I used a candle.)
- Strong magnets (if you want)

Step 2: Make the Body

Cut out a piece of wire that is double the height that you want your person to be. Bend the middle of the wire around the round thing you found to make the head. You don't need it, but it will make your person look better. Bend out the legs.

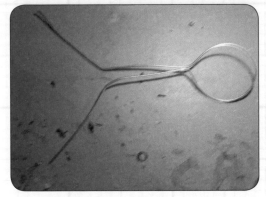

Step 3: Make the Arms

Cut a piece of wire that is as long as 2 arms. Bend it around the body and flatten it with the wire cutters (see picture).

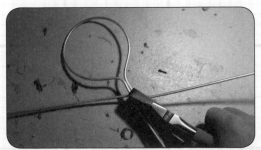

Step 4: Tape 'er Up

Now it is time to use your duct tape skills. Before you start taping you might need to trim the arms or legs so they are even.

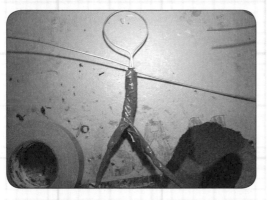

Step 5: Finished!

Now you should add more duct tape to the arms and legs to even them up. Make another one to have even more fun!

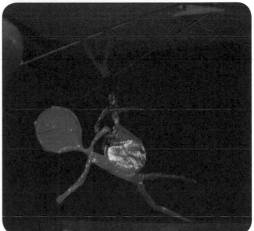

Duct Tape Giraffe
By digwells
www.instructables.com/id/Duct-Tape-
Giraffe-Tall-and-Self-Supported/

This guide will teach you how to make a large giraffe out of only duct tape and sweat (preferably not on the poor creature itself). It will turn heads and score big when it comes to presents.

Step 1: Gather the Forces
For this you will need:
- 2–3 rolls of duct tape (one color for the base, one for the spots, and one that can be used as backing for the sheets—explanation later)
- X-Acto knife/box cutter (I find X-Acto knife works best) and scissors
- Ruler (I use an 18-inch ruler because of the mat size)
- Cutting mat (I use a 36-inch x 20-inch but a 12-inch x 16-inch will do too. Or any size for that matter.)
- An old magazine
- ½-inch piece of dowel or a drill bit

Step 2: Duct Tape Sheets
The duct tape sheet is the basis for any duct tape project and is indeed important here. Duct tape is composed of threads dipped in adhesive rubbers. Basically, you will be making the "fabric" for this grand project.
1. To make the "fabric" for the legs, you'll want to make a 16-inch x 10-inch sheet. Lay down strips of the base-color tape color-side up, overlapping the left edge of the tape about a centimeter over the right edge of the adjacent tape.
2. This is the tricky part—peel from the bottom left corner. Once you have this side completed, slowly, as to not wrinkle the tape too much (and, yes, it does wrinkle), flip it over on the mat with the sticky side now facing up. (Also, make sure not to have the tape stick to itself. It could cause havoc for you.)
3. Take your third roll (or if you decide you have enough, the same color), cut strips 12 inches long, and begin to add the second side. The edges should now all be facing left and you should begin laying the strips down beginning on the left. This will make a strong seam. Also, be sure of your placement. The time it takes to peel duct tape off it itself is quite long and could end in you restarting and wasting tape. Put your finished sheet aside.
4. Repeat steps 1 through 3, but make a 10-inch x 4-inch sheet for the neck and a 6-inch x 5-inch for the body.

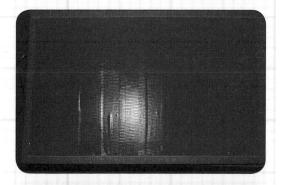

the center lengthwise and making a cut every ½ inch or so usually does the trick.

1. Cut the 16-inch x 10-inch sheet into four 4-inch x 10-inch sections. Each one will be one leg. Roll the sheet around your ½-inch dowel or bit and put a pin in it at the base, one at the other end, and one in the center. Remove the piece from the dowel. Do this for the other 3 also.
2. Take 4 of your pins and connect the 2 ends of the body pieces together.
3. With the same process used for the legs, make the neck cloth.

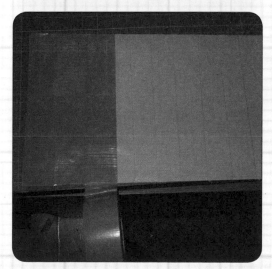

Step 3: The Cuts and Rolls

Now that you have all of the necessary sheets, snip snip!

Prior to step 1, lay down a strip of your base color that you will use as your "pins," or the tape you use to keep things in place. Cutting it down

Step 5: Stuffing the Legs and Neck

Even though a pure duct tape giraffe would be fun, it couldn't hold its own weight. Tear out pages from your magazine and proceed to stuff each limb to a logical point. You want it firm but not too full. It's a discreet stuffing. Use the other side of your X-Acto knife to force the paper down to fill the leg. Two pages per leg should do. Also, fill the neck.

Step 4: Closing the Seams

The trick to having a standing giraffe is to add stuffing inside the all the body parts. And the trick to making people take this large creation seriously is not making it look like duct tape, which means covering all your edges. But that's why you're reading this.

Roll out three 10-inch strips and cut them in half. Place one strip on the seam of each leg. Also, with the leftover strip, cover the seam of the body and cut off the extra.

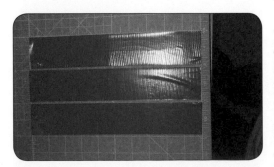

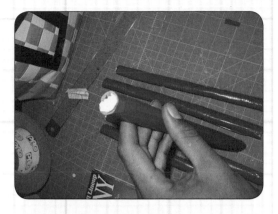

Step 6: Filling the Body

The body is a little more fun to fill. A rule to keep in mind for anything tape related that you don't want wrinkles in is to just make a little cut wherever you think it might stick to itself. That way, instead of sticking to itself and making the dreaded crease, it simply overlaps. This will be relevant shortly.

1. Lay down a 4-inch x 4-inch square of tape, then flip it over.
2. Stick one end of the open body on it.
3. Fill the body with magazine pages until full.
4. After you've filled the body, make slits in the tape like you were cutting the rays of sunshine around a sun.
5. Fold each piece up until the end is completely closed. Be sure to cut enough to avoid any wrinkles, sticky sides, and sticking together.
6. Make another 4-inch x 4-inch square and put the unfinished side of the body down and do the same thing.

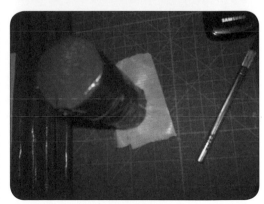

Step 7: Closing the Legs

Use the same sunshine-beam technique, but with a more suitable-sized piece of tape, to close up the leg ends. You only need to close one side, which will then turn into the feet. I would give dimensions, but I know that no two duct tape projects turn out exactly the same, so use your best judgment. Close one end of every leg. Leave the neck piece open on both ends.

Step 8: Attaching the Legs

1. Cut a 1-inch x 1-inch piece of tape, just like the picture shows.
2. Attach the piece to the top of the leg, as in the picture.
3. Then put it so the top of the leg is flat against the bottom edge of the giraffe and attach the tape. It should fold over because of the slit.
4. Cut another square, but this time, do the mirror-image cuts, because the edge is now on the other side. Just make sure that the flap is pointing out.
5. Reinforce the inside crack of the leg to prevent them from detaching and continue to do the other set of legs the same way.

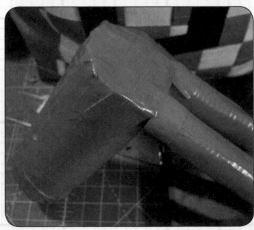

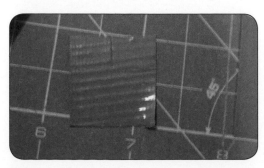

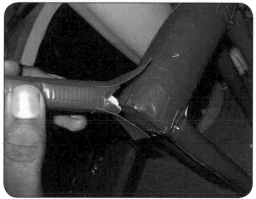

Step 9: Attaching the Neck and Head

1. Pick up the uncapped neck and cut a V out of it.
2. Cut a 3-inch piece of tape in half and place one strip on the top and another on the bottom of the neck.
3. Place the neck on the giraffe as shown. Push down the tape strips firmly, and then add another 3-inch piece perpendicular to the base where the neck meets the body for reinforcement.
4. Start rolling the end of your tape on itself until it's about as big as the ½-inch piece you have. Cut the ends so you have a nice flush surface and make 2 more sunshine pieces to cover the end. You roll the tape much like you would a cigarette. Make sure the tape is tightly rolled.
5. Attach the head with a piece of tape on each side and one on the back, making the back of the head flush with the neck.

Step 10: Covering Your Work

Covering all of the gross seams and folds is the very important part. I've worked hard to make my stuff and this project look the best it can.

1. Make a piece of tape long enough to cover each leg. Make sure some of it attaches to the body to add stability.
2. The cut points are key to avoiding any wrinkles, which we are trying to cover up. The pictures will be the most helpful thing at this point. Any place where it could fold in on itself or where there will be a gap under the tape should have a cut point. Like I said—see pictures.
3. After the legs are covered, make strips to lie horizontally on the body. Pictures for the cut points are probably most helpful at this stage.
4. Cut a round piece in the shape of the front and back to cover up the overlapping pieces.
5. In summary, short jagged pieces hurt the eyes, creases and wrinkles are hard to cut off,

any pieces that have space under them aren't good. Try to make it look as clean and neat as possible.

Step 11: Adding the Spots

For those of you who ventured this far, you still have a journey ahead. For me this part takes as much time, if not longer, than every step before this. The only thing that turns this long-legged, tall-necked horse into a giraffe is the spots. These will fit together like one big sticky puzzle. I have pictures to demonstrate. You can also freestyle if you like; your creativity can do what it pleases. Whatever you choose to do has to fit together, giving the "giraffe" look.

Put down a 16-inch x 12-inch sheet of the second the roll of tape you got for the spots. Start from the center and start cutting out this elaborate puzzle. Take it out piece by piece and start attaching it, beginning at the most central point so it spreads out from the top and center of the body.

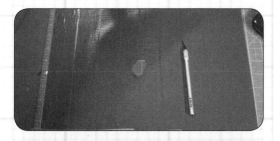

Step 12: Finishing Details

Finally, now that you've made it through the woods, we just need to add a mane, eyes, tail, and those antler-horn things.

1. The mane involves cutting a 10-inch piece of tape in half hot-dog style and folding it over with some open tape still showing. Cut little lines all the way down the thing, being careful only to cut the folded part and not the sticky stuff.
2. Add the antlers, which is really just taking random scraps and folding them over enough, leaving some sticky like you did with the mane. You could even just cut off 2 pieces from the mane.
3. The tail is just a rolled sheet of duct tape like you did with the head, but much smaller. Stick that to tail end (pun) of the giraffe with a small piece of tape that matches the spot you are placing it on, or if you're sticking it to the body, use the base color.
4. The eyes are just small squares of the base color.

about it. And if it turned out better than you hoped, you've got the knack for tape. You can change the dimensions, change the size, change colors, do whatever you want. So have fun with it, it's tape!

Step 13: The Finished Product

After a couple hours of work your giraffe will be completed. I know for me my first ones were not the same quality that they are today. So if it didn't turn out how you hoped, don't even worry

Emergency Stuffed Animal

By sourpersimmons
www.instructables.com/id/Emergency-
Stuffed-Animal/

Feeling lonely but don't want to be around people? Wish you had something inanimate to hug, but can't afford those pricey large stuffed animals? Want something like this *right now*? Then check this out! It takes around an hour and costs under $5!

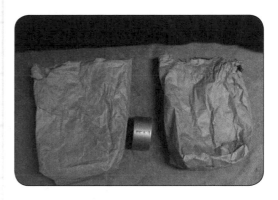

Step 1: Materials

All you really need to make this stuffed animal are 2 paper bags and a roll of duct tape. Smaller paper bags work best, and make sure to crumple them up beforehand to make them nice and soft. You may need 2 rolls of duct tape depending on how precise you are.

Not pictured is a pair of scissors and a Sharpie to draw the face on in the end. Optionally, you can also use cotton balls to fill in the gaps and make it a bit softer, but you can get by just fine without them.

Step 2: Crumple

First things first, take one of the paper bags and crumple it into an oblong shape. You can make it more rectangular or triangular depending on what you want your end result to look like.

Step 3: Add Duct Tape

Next, take a few long strips of duct tape and wrap them around the paper bag to stabilize the shape. Don't worry about how it looks right now; you just want to make sure it holds together for the time being.

Step 4: Cover the Bag

Now, work on covering up all the bits of paper bag that are still showing. When you get to the bottom and top of the oblong shape, use shorter strips of duct tape, since they will lie flat easier than the long ones.

Step 5: Keep Wrapping

Keep wrapping the shape in duct tape until you've flattened down all the bits that stick up. When you're done, you should have something that looks like this:

Step 6: The Head

Now that the body is done, it's time for the head. Crumple up the other paper bag, but this time, make it a shorter shape that will work better as a head. Then just repeat what you did for the body.

Step 7: Attach Head

Once the head is done, you can put it on the body. Use a lot of short strips that will lie flat and make a nice smooth joining. You could also use a little bit of glue just to be absolutely sure the head won't fall off, but it's really not necessary.

Step 8: The Ears

To make the ears, just take a medium strip of duct tape and fold one corner over so that it makes a triangle. Do the same for the other side so that you have 2 triangles together. Use a few more strips to strengthen the ears, but be sure not to put any tape over the crease in the middle or the ears won't fold properly.

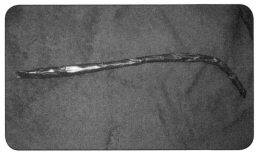

Step 9: Attach Ears

Attach the ears much the same way you attached the head, except use smaller pieces of duct tape. Tape both the front and back of the ear so that it will stay attached. Repeat the process for the second ear.

Step 11: Nearly Done

Alright, you should have something that looks like the photo below by now. Almost done!

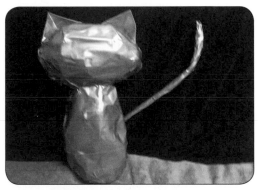

Step 12: Add a Face

Now all that's left is to draw a face on it. Go wild with this—you could make it cute, sad, angry, whatever you want. And if you mess up or just want to change its face later, all you need to do is put a strip or 2 of duct tape over it and you'll have a blank canvas to work with again.

Enjoy your extremely cheap and surprisingly cuddly new stuffed animal!

Step 10: The Tail

To make the tail, just take a really long strip of duct tape and twist it up so it makes a sort of rope. Then cover it in smaller strips of duct tape until it's as thick as you want it to be. To make the curve at the end of the tail, use much smaller strips of duct tape while curving the tail in the direction you want. Then just tape it to the back of the body with a piece of duct tape, and it should hold just fine.

This project teaches you how to make adorable duct tape pets!

Step 1: Supplies You'll Need

- Duct tape (whatever colors you want to make your pets)
- Scissors or a rotary knife
- Ruler

Step 3: The Tail

You can make the tail as long as you want. The model is 1½ inches long and ½ inch wide. Fold the strip in half the long way. Then take a strip the same width and attach it to the body.

Step 2: The Body

You'll want a piece of tape 4 inches long and 2 inches wide. If you want your pet to be one color 2 strips should do it. For 2 different colors use 2 different colored strips. With 3 colors, you'll need to cut the strips to size.

Note: Cut the strips double the length above.

Fold one strip width wise. Then attach the second strip to the first and fold it width wise half over the first one. See photos.

Step 4: Eyes

Eyes, in my opinion, are the hardest part. Take a color and cut a small piece. Cut away the corners until the eye is roundish. Then take another color and do the same, but smaller, and place the smaller one on top of the first one to be the pupil.

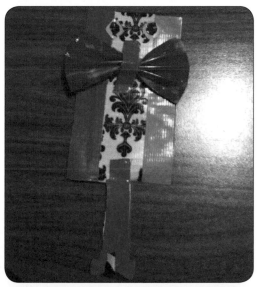

Step 5: Accessorizing

You can add bows or maybe use string for hair. You could cut a slit in its tail to make it look like a snake tongue. Any way you do it, they are adorable!

Extra Fun

Duct Tape Easter Basket

By DuctTapeExtremeDude
www.instructables.com/id/
Duct-Tape-Easter-Basket/

My sister inspired me to make this Easter basket.

Step 1: Materials
First, you will need:
- A cardboard box
- 2 or more rolls of duct tape of different colors
- A tape measure
- A pocket knife or other small knife
- A pencil
- A ruler

Step 2: Starting to Cut
First, measure how wide your roll of duct tape is. Then mark that length 6 times and make 6 rectangles (see picture). To make the rectangles

exact, follow the lines on the cardboard. Then make a line across the tops of the rectangles to make them into 6 boxes that are 5 inches by how wide your duct tape is. Now cut them out.

Step 3: Continuing
Now measure along a crease in your cardboard and make 12 marks, each one inch apart. Make 12 rectangles, and make 6 of them 5 inches long, and the other six 6 inches long. Cut them out.

Step 4: Finish Cutting

Now find a part of your cardboard that's at least 25 inches long. Make 3 marks on it that are each 1¼ inches apart (see picture). Now make 2 long strips that are each 1¼ inches x 25 inches long. Cut them out.

Step 5: Stop and Double Check

Now stop and check to make sure you have all the parts. You should have:

- 6 pieces that are 5 inches x the width of your duct tape (A pieces)
- 6 parts that are 1 inch x 5 inches (B pieces)
- 6 pieces that are 1 inch x 6 inches (C pieces)
- 2 pieces that are 1¼ inches x 25 inches (D pieces)

Step 6: Start the Frame

Now bend all the A pieces down the middle. Use your ruler to get a straight line. Now take 2 B pieces and put them on a piece of duct tape as shown. Now tape them to a bent piece so that they hang down on each side. Now tape another B piece on one of the ends. Put a bent piece on that and tape it the same way you taped the other one. Do it again until you have only one bent piece and no B pieces.

Step 7: Finish the Frame

Now bend the big piece you have made around and tape the last bent piece onto it. Now take a C piece and put it up against the top of the frame (see picture) and memorize the angle it's at against the top of the frame (see picture).

Tape it to the top of the frame. Tape another C piece onto the frame next to the other piece (see picture). Now tape another C piece onto the frame in the same way. Do the same all the way around the frame. The finished frame should look like it does in the picture on the following page.

Step 8: Beginning to Decorate

Now measure out a strip of a different color duct tape that's 40 inches long. Cut it off and fold it in half. It's okay if it has minor wrinkles, as it's nearly impossible to keep it totally smooth. Now make another. Tape an end to a bent piece in the frame, making sure it's about ¼ inch away from the top (see picture). Keeping it tight, wind it around the frame, keeping it the same distance from the top the entire way around. Then tape the other end onto the frame, next to the first end. Cut off the excess. Now do it again with the other strip of duct tape, except next to the bottom of the frame. It should now look like the picture.

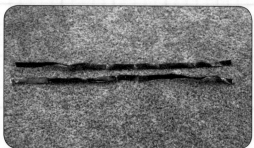

Step 9: Continued

Now cut a strip of duct tape that's a little longer than your frame is high. Put it on one of the bent pieces, over the strips of colored duct tape. Make sure the colored duct tape is at the right height before you tape it. Do the same on all the other corners. Then put it on the inside of the corners. It should now look like the picture.

Step 10: Add the Walls

Now take a strip of colored duct tape that's between 4 inches and 5 inches and fold it over to get a thinner strip. Make more until you have 12 strips. Take a piece of duct tape but don't cut it off of the roll. Tape it onto the top of the frame all the way around. As you put it on, use it to tape the strips over the gaps in the wall, 2 for each gap (see picture). At each corner you will need to make a small wrinkle to get it to point the right way to cover the cardboard. When you've gone all the way around, cut the strip off the roll and fold it over the top of the basket. Don't worry about the huge wrinkles you'll make; we'll fix that in the next step.

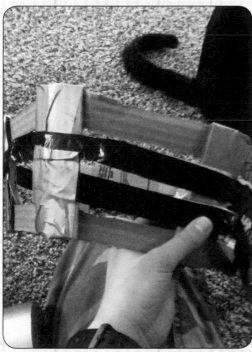

175

Step 11: Removing Huge Wrinkles

Cut the end of your duct tape in half. Now take off a strip that's half as wide as your duct tape and about 18 inches long. Put it around half of the inside of your basket so that it covers the wrinkles and any exposed cardboard. To finish the upper part of your basket, weave the strips in the walls together. Do not tape them to the base of the frame.

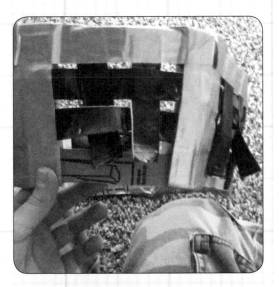

Step 12: Make the Bottom

Now make 6 strips of colored duct tape that are 10 inches long, and 4 strips that are 8 inches long. Weave the 10 inch strips together as shown. Then weave the 8 inch strips into the sides to get a rough circle. Now put tape on it in a hexagon shape. Peel it off the floor and tape a hexagon shape onto the other side so that no stickiness is showing.

Step 13: Finish the Body

First, set the frame onto the bottom of the basket and use a pencil to make dents at the corners (see picture). Then cut the bottom to that size. Now put a strip of duct tape all the way around the base of the basket, making sure to tape the strips of the walls into place. Cut a slit in the strip at each of the corners. Now tape the bottom of the basket in as shown. Flip the basket over and tape the bottom on the inside as shown. Your basket should now look like the picture.

Step 14: The Handle

Now take your 25-inch strips (D strips from earlier) and cover one side with a strip of duct tape as shown. Now cover the other side and fold down the edges. Now cut the end of your colored duct tape in half and wrap one side around the handle as shown. Halfway down the handle, stop and use the other side of the strip. This will ensure you have a normal end on your duct tape roll when you are done. There should be no wrinkles on the handle. When you are done, bend the handle so that it curves, as shown.

Step 15: Finish the Basket

Now put a half strip of duct tape on the handle. Tape the handle onto the basket as shown. Take another half strip and tape it on as shown. Now take 2 more strips and tape them over the ends of the last piece. Do the same on the other side.

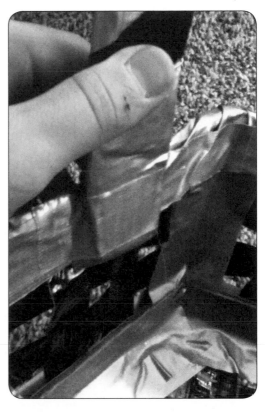

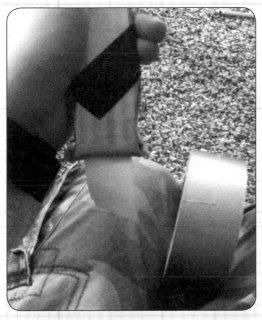

Step 16: Now You're Done!

Now you have a nice, strong basket that you can keep or give away. It's strong, so it can be used for more than just Easter.

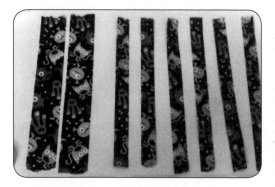

Step 1: You'll Need 2 Simple Things

Duct tape and scissors! Although, you will not need scissors if you rip your duct tape.

Step 2: Cutting and Folding

Cut 8 pieces of duct tape that are 1 foot each, then fold 6 of the pieces in half, leaving the other two as they are for now.

Step 3: Make Your "Skeleton"

Put your folded pieces in the shape of a star. First make a cross, and then add strips in between and around. It has to be even.

Step 4: Tape Your Skeleton

Follow the images to tape your skeleton.

182

Step 5: Time to Use Your Seventh and Eighth Strips

Cut them into quarters. These will connect your skeleton and make the bowl.

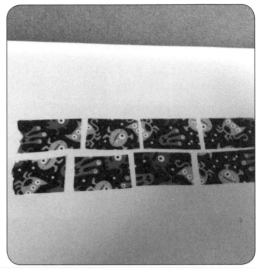

Step 6: Connecting Your Skeleton

Connect a strip to the next, making it curved. I think that the first connection is the hardest, so it will be easier as you go along. If you need more pieces for sticking, cut more.

Step 7: Covering the Outside

Be careful! Your bowl right now is very fragile! Pat the strips down gently. After you cover the inside, you can use your hand and push the rest down.

Step 8: Covering the Inside

Make sure the lumps are gone! Just put strips inside until you see no sticky parts.

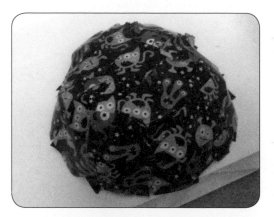

Step 9: Trim It

Trim your bowl. Finished!

Here is a way to place designs and patterns on your duct tape projects without risk of them peeling or rubbing off. This raised image will remain in place despite the wear of everyday use. It is perfect for adding an extra piece of flair to any project.

Step 1: The Design

After you have picked your design, create a piece of tape with no exposed sticky side. This is done by sandwiching together 2 pieces of tape.

Make sure this tape is larger than the design you want to use.

Once you have this base, sketch out the design on its surface. Do not worry over bad lines or erasing, as this part will not be seen in the finished product. When laying down your design, keep in mind that small gaps may not show up in the end, so it might help to widen those areas if possible.

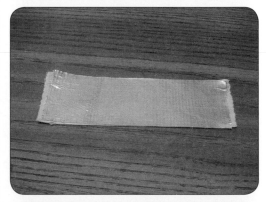

Step 2: Cutting

Once you have your pattern in place, start cutting it out. If you make a mistake cutting, it is not the end of the world. If you align the 2 halves the cut will not show up when you're finished. This is helpful when getting to open areas in the middle of your design.

Step 3: Setting It In

Now that you have your design cut out, it is time to insert it into your project. Lay out a strip of tape with the sticky side up and place the figure on top of it. Lay down more tape on top of the whole thing, sticky side down, and sandwich the design in. Now, using the fleshy part of your finger, press in the tape around the edges of the figure. This should leave a raised, defined shape in the face of the tape.

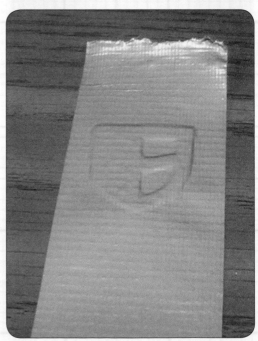

Step 4: Versatility

The area of embossed tape you've made can be integrated into many tape projects or become a piece all its own. Your images can be as simple or complex as you can manage.

This will show you how to make a collapsible cup out of duct tape. This is great for camping, hiking, and traveling.

Step 1: Supplies

You will need:

- Duct tape
- Cutting utensil (X-Acto knife works best)
- Ruler or measuring tape

Step 2: Bottom Ring

To make the bottom ring/the base of the cup:

1. Cut a piece of tape 7–8 inches long.
2. Fold the piece of tape in half lengthwise, or hotdog style.
3. Bend it into a ring shape and tape it so that it stays in that shape.

Step 3: Second Ring

Make the second ring:

1. Measure out a piece of tape by lining your tape up with the first ring and marking with your finger how long it should be so that it fits snuggly.
2. Cut wherever you marked.
3. Fold in half lengthwise, or hotdog style.
4. Wrap that around the first ring (first ring is blue, second is gray in the photo).
5. Tape at the joint where the ring connects. DO NOT TAPE TO THE INSIDE RING.
6. Slide the inside ring out.
7. Finish taping the second/outside ring.
8. Slide the outside ring back on.
9. Keep using the same process. Remember: Use the second ring to measure the third ring, the third ring to measure the fourth ring, etc., like a telescope.

Step 5: Finishing the Cup

Insert the bottom back into the cup and you are finished—you have a collapsible cup!

Step 4: Base/Bottom of the Cup

1. Cut 2 pieces of duct tape that are longer than the diameter of the bottom ring of your cup. My cup could fit on one piece. If yours can't, cut 2 more pieces the same size.
2. If you only have one piece, just stick the 2 sticky sides on top of each other.
3. If you needed 2 pieces, place one piece sticky side up. Put a piece sticky side up on the edge of that. Place the other 2 pieces on top of those.
4. Trace your bottom ring onto the non-sticky piece of tape you just made.
5. Cut out where you traced.
6. Tape to the bottom of your first ring.
7. Re-cover the sides and bottom of the ring with tape.

As I was putting up my Christmas tree, I realized it was *way* too bare. I, being my normal cheap self, needed to create a cheap, fun way to decorate my tree. And so I did. I introduce to you the Duct Tape Ornament. And the great thing about it is that you can find some use for it during all the seasons, maybe as a door knob accessory.

Step 1: What You Will Need
- Yarn (whatever color fits your needs)
- Scissors
- Duct tape (preferably colored)
- Any ball-like object that fits your desired size (I went with a tennis ball)

Step 2: Getting Started
Start off by cutting around 6 inches of yarn to use as the hanger. Simply tape the yarn to whatever side of the ball-like object you choose to be the top. Now, on the direct other side of the ball, tape an outline of a nice, big square in whatever color it is that you are going to start with (I used black).

Step 3: How to Design
Now, to design the ball the way I did, I used the same technique used with making duct tape roses. It's simple to make yet creates decent designs. Start by taking some duct tape around 2 inches long, or whatever length creates a square piece of duct tape. Fold end over end to give it a triangle look with tape exposed at the bottom.

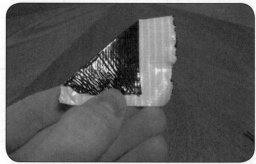

Step 4: Applying the Design

Starting from the bottom, ring the ball with the triangle shapes. I did mine by levels, alternating colors as I went up. Don't worry about the bottom of the ball, because it's okay to show the bottom a bit. In fact, when you're done with the first level, it should vaguely remind you of a jet engine. (That's how I saw it at least.) When you are going up on the levels, keep making the same amount of triangles, because you will begin to think that you can't fit them all as you keep going up, but you can. It looks better if you do so. To clean up the top, basically, just apply the color of tape that you started with around the hanger using small bits of tape. Be sure not to leave any places that don't clean up well.

Step 5: Tree Ornament or Home Decor

Whatever you choose to do with your newly made duct tape ornament, have fun with your design. I showed you how I made mine, but I'm sure any of you could easily improve the design. Get creative! This can even make a great gift because you can even use it as a ceiling fan pull chain ball or put it on your door, or maybe even just make tons of them and tape them to your bedroom ceiling. Get out there and show the world your new talent!

also available

Loom Magic!
25 Awesome, Never-Before-Seen Designs for an Amazing Rainbow of Projects

John McCann and Becky Thomas

This book includes twenty-five new rubber band loom projects, including bracelets, sports-themed charms, key rings, pendants, and even a working slingshot. New crafters and dedicated fans will enjoy creating the wide variety of projects in this collection, including:

- Cell phone case
- Daisy chain bracelet
- Watch band
- Octo bracelet
- Blooming beaded bracelet
- Sports fan keychain
- Matching barrettes

- Pencil topper
- Rainbow ring
- Nunchuks
- Rocker cuff bracelet
- Snowman ornament
- And many more!

US $12.95 hardcover ISBN: 978-1-62914-334-7

also available

Loom Magic Creatures!
25 Awesome Animals and Mythical Beings for a Rainbow of Critters

Becky Thomas and Monica Sweeney

From the authors of bestselling titles *Loom Magic!* and *Loom Magic Xtreme!* comes *Loom Magic Creatures!: 25 Awesome Animals and Mythical Beings for a Rainbow of Critters*. According to the *New York Times*, Rainbow Looms are the hottest trend on the market, and it is continuously growing in popularity. New and crazy designs are being created every day, and now you can astound all of your friends with these fun and wacky critters, including:

- Medusa
- Butterfly
- Penguin
- Crab
- Dog
- Bunny
- Spider
- Pig

- Gingerbread man
- Parrot
- Dragon
- Princess
- Santa
- Robot
- Cat
- And many more!

This collection of never-before-seen projects will have all of your friends begging for your Rainbow Loom secrets!

US $12.95 hardcover ISBN: 978-1-62914-795-6

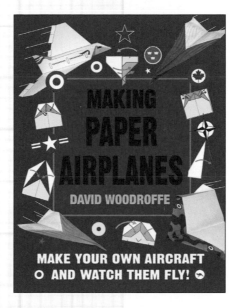

Making Paper Airplanes
Make Your Own Aircraft and Watch Them Fly!

David Woodroffe

Now anyone can turn a stack of paper into their own private air force. Packed with diagrams, instructions, and graphics, here are amazing paper aircraft that really fly—origami fighter jets, helicopters, and more. Customized graphics for each model ensure that your aircraft will look great and fly better than any paper plane you have ever folded. All of the fantastic flying machines featured have been built and tested by the author to ensure that, with little more than a few folds and a couple of snips, your new creation can get airborne. This is a great activity book for family and friends of all ages and bright summer days.

US $12.95 paperback ISBN: 978-1-62087-168-3

What's the BIG Idea?
Amazing Science Questions for the Curious Kid
Vicki Cobb

Why does a rolling ball stop rolling? Why doesn't the sun burn out? Why can't you unscramble an egg? Why can't we live forever? These are all questions that a curious kid might ask. In *What's the BIG Idea?*, renowned juvenile science educator Vicki Cobb answers these and thirty-one other fascinating questions to help kids learn more about the world through the wonders of science.

A big idea is one that has no simple or easy answer, and there are four big ideas in this book: motion, energy, matter, and life. The motion of nonliving objects—rolling balls, falling stones, the moon and stars—seems so ordinary and familiar that most people take it for granted. Matter, on the other hand, comes in so many different forms—solids, liquids, gases, metals, nonmetals, living material—it is hard to imagine anything that all matter has in common. Energy is an idea that is in the news just about every day, yet most people couldn't tell you what the big idea of energy is. And life seems mind-boggling and infinitely complicated. How do we bend our brains around it?

Scientists learn by asking questions. And *What's the BIG Idea?* is designed to make young readers stop and think about each of the thirty-five questions before reading what scientists have learned that answers each question. They'll be able to do simple things to see for themselves and build their own scientific knowledge in the process. By the time they've finished this book, they'll have a pretty good idea of what science is all about.

US $12.95 paperback ISBN: 978-1-62087-685-5